Buttered-Side Down

A COOKBOOK FOR THE EMANCIPATED MALE

BUTTERED-SIDE DOWN

A COOKBOOK FOR THE EMANCIPATED MALE

Buttered - Side Down

A COOKBOOK FOR THE EMANCIPATED MALE

B. J. Verts

ISBN 0-9745769-0-5

Published by Verts Creations
WWW.VERTSCREATIONS.COM

Printed in United States

9 8 7 6 5 4 3 2 1

The paper used in this publication meets the minimum
requirements of American National Standards for Information
Sciences—Permanence of Paper for Printed Library
Materials, ANZI Z39.48-1984.

TABLE OF CONTENTS

page

4-quart Pressure Cooker

3 sizes of Sauce Pans

6-quart Stock Pot

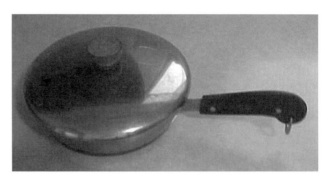

Frying pan

Dutch Oven

Wok with lid

Cookie Sheet

PREFACE

This cookbook is based largely on experiences derived from surviving after having become a "new" single. For 20+ years of marriage, the kitchen was off limits. If I were hungry, I asked for a sandwich or complained that dinner was overdue. Magically, I was fed. I knew that mayonnaise and butter were applied with a knife, and that the side of the bread to which they were applied invariably was the side that came in contact with the floor or counter top when the bread was dropped. This knowledge came from tears of anguish shed by my ex-wife who, while preparing a tray of open-faced little sandwiches for a party early in our marriage, accidently dumped the lot on a newly scrubbed and waxed kitchen floor. Hence, the deriviation of the name for this cookbook.

Upon becoming single again, I had a partly furnished house, a Ph.D. in Zoology (probably not much of an asset), and damned little money (fortunately not in the debit column), but an intense desire to "make it on my own." My teen-age son, although a sophmore in college, continued to live at home for the first year. However, he was unable to contribute to the success of my new-found adventure other than to stand around with his mouth open like a baby robin waiting to be fed. Hunger, and my son's incessant chirping, ultimately led me to overcome my reluctance to enter the domain from which I had been excluded for so long.

I had no cookbook. I didn't know how to turn on the broiler (had I known what it was for) or even the dishwasher (from the name, I understood its role). I knew that foodstuffs from the freezer kept until thawed, but I did not know how to thaw them safely. I had no microwave—and after legal fees and the divorce settlement, no hope of purchasing one. I had a cabinet full of spices and herbs, but had to taste each one to gain an understanding of how they might be used. A pinch of red pepper on my tongue ended my experiments with herbs for several hours.

A grocery advertisement for "blade-cut pot roast" included a sketch depicting a cut of meat with potatoes, onions, and carrots along side. Meat, potatoes, and some other vegetables seemed a reasonably balanced diet after peanut butter, crackers, and milk for 3 days. The artist's rendition stimulated excessive salivation all the way to the grocery. I was disallusioned when I learned that "blade-cut pot roasts" in the grocery were not packaged with appropriate quantities of potatoes, onions, and carrots as shown in the advertisement. I was careful to pick a pot roast with the configuration of the bone as close as possible to that depicted in the advertisement. Finding carrots, onions, and potatoes was a breeze—they were all on a counter with a lot of green stuff. The anxiety of the first trip to the grocery reached a crescendo with the writing of the first check in a check-out lane. Four matronly women and the check-out lady leered at the unsuntanned quarter-inch-wide band on the third finger of my left hand and exchanged knowing glances. I changed my mind about asking the check-out lady how to cook a "blade-cut pot roast."

I don't recall the last meal that my ex-wife cooked for which she used the oven, but I shall be forever grateful that she left the temperature dial set on 350°F. I attempted to prepare the newly purchased foodstuffs in a manner to duplicate that shown in the advertisement. I quartered the potatoes and onions, but peeled neither as the sketch was not too clear on the point. However, as the sketch did not show green tops on the carrots, they were duly lopped off. The tops make simply awful salads. Vegetables and meat were placed in a wide flat pan—later found to be a cake pan—and that placed in the oven and a dial on top of the stove marked "OVEN" turned to the "ON" position.

Over the years, I had developed a "fixed-action pattern" for feeding my springer spaniels. At precisely 5:30 p.m. they barked. Immediately and totally without thinking, I rinsed 2 pans under the faucet at the south side of the house, left half-inch of water in each, added 2 scoops of dry dog food to each, and served 1 to each dog. If feeding 2 dogs could be so easy, surely I could master the art of feeding 2 people. However, that evening on the way from the kennel after feeding the dogs, I tarried to replace the cable on the winch used to pull the dory onto the trailer. This led to a few other minor repairs that required about 2 hours. The hunger pangs started again and that reminded me of the "blade-cut pot roast" that should be nearly ready.

The roast and vegetables didn't look quite as they were depicted in the grocery advertisement! With the aid of a wide-blade putty knife and my son to hold the cake pan, I extracted most of what was left of the roast. Little remained of the vegetables, and what remained had the distinct flavor of charcoal. Nevertheless, we ingested the results of my first venture into the kitchen with gusto, even though the "blade-cut pot roast" required considerable mastication—and considerable effort to masticate.

From this humble culinary beginning, advancement came quickly (as survival was dependent thereon, it could hardly be otherwise). I began to read recipes in newspapers and magazines (the women's magazines to which my ex-wife subscribed still were delivered to my house; I would have never had the courage at that stage of my emancipation to subscribe to them myself). A friend, who I invited to the first dinner that I cooked for someone other than my son took pity on me and bought me a basic and elementary cookbook. As with all people who work, time for cooking is extremely limited; I quickly learned to ignore recipes that required more than 2 pans for preparation or more than 30 minutes to cook, or to prepare dishes that could be cooked without constant attention. From these experiences, I developed some fundamental laws regarding the preparation of food:

1. NO RECIPE IS CARVED IN STONE. One of the most rewarding aspects of cooking is the alteration of recipes to fit your particular taste. The ratio of liquid to dry material shouldn't be mucked around with too much, but spices, flavorings, and other items (discussed in individual recipes) can be changed to fit your mood. Keep a record of how you alter recipes so that you can remember to include what you like, and omit the less palatable.

2. SOME FLAVORS ARE INCOMPATIBLE. This was driven home by Sybil, a girl friend who knew less about cooking that I, who seasoned a meatloaf with copious amounts of ground cinnamon. The object of the art is to try small amounts of new or different herbs and spices to determine if flavors titillate or turn off the palate. At least, such an approach will not result in excessive amounts of food rendered unetible (a concern of some consequence if there is a baby robin in the household). Sybil's meatloaf, made with *my* hamburger, was not salvagable; Sybil's dogs that normally ate anything digestable in fuming nitric acid were somewhat reluctant to consume it.

3. COOKING TEMPERATURE AND TIME ARE MORE CRITICAL THAN AMOUNTS OF ITEMS INCLUDED IN MOST DISHES. With a minimum of experimentation, I learned that "blade-cut post roast" (I still couldn't afford a better cut of beef) was best cooked in a moderate (350°F) oven uncovered for about 45 minutes, the vegetables added, and the whole lot covered and cooked for another 45 minutes. (Such a procedure also reduced mastication time and effort, and eliminated the charcoal taste in the vegetables). Later, I learned that overcooking reduces both the nutritive value and palatability of many foods, especially vegetables. No wonder I hated broccoli as a child—my mother boiled it for half an hour!

4. THE KEY TO SUCCESSFUL COOKING AND MEAL PREPARATION LIES IN TIMING. Just as the comic's key to telling a joke successfully, the components of a meal must all come together at the proper moment if it is to be a successful meal. So, at least at the onset, it is necessary to become intimately familiar with the timing device on the stove (and you must stay within earshot of whatever signal it produces). In addition, each stove cooks at a bit different speed, an axiom that I learned by experience when my beloved electric with manual dials had to be replaced with a digital model. I blamed the overcooked food on my clumsiness in programing the timer, but, in truth, the old oven had gaskets that leaked heat, so my old oven cooked more slowly than my new one. Soon, however, a sixth sense replaces the dependence on the timer and it is possible to know automatically when steaming the potatoes must commence if they are to be mashed and ready at the same time that the rump roast will be done (note the advancement from "blade-cut pot roast").

5. DO WHATEVER YOU CAN TO GET SOMEONE ELSE TO CLEAN UP THE MESS. By the time that my son decided to try to make a go of it on his own, I had become sufficiently skilled in the art of cooking that our survival was no longer in doubt. But being left alone, I could no longer strut about after preparing a particularly palatable meal and attempt to make him feel sufficiently guilty to take care of the dishes and to clean the kitchen. I induced a series of girl friends to partake of my culinary skills so that I might stay in practice and to tempt them with new delicacies, but few indeed offered to do the dishes and clean my kitchen. Finally, it came to the point that there was no other way but marriage. During courtship, my bride-to-be ate my food with gusto and complimented my skills, and even occasionally rewarded me by doing the dishes and cleaning my kitchen. However, upon learning that I had come to enjoy being the cook and was willing to continue in that capacity after marriage, she immediately forgot everything that she had ever known about preparation of meals and became an expert at skullery duty. Rarely does she complain about the number of pots and pans that I use in the preparation of a meal, so I suppose that she has concluded that a trade-off is better than having to do the whole works: plan meals, do the shopping, prepare and cook food, and clean up afterwards. So, mates, learning to cook will not only insure your survival in times of need, but might, just might, become the asset that attracts a new spouse to assume the less attractive aspects of meal preparation. And, as culinary specialist, you get all the glory!

When I decided to write a cookbook and survival manual, my original plan was to compile my best recipes, describe a few alternatives, and let it go at that. My problem was that I had some difficulty recalling my state of knowledge regarding cooking some 28+ years ago when I became a new single. Also, changes in health with age, and in knowledge regarding what constitutes a healthful diet, required alterations of numerous recipes to conform to my physician's demands. So, I have decided to provide my best recipes as altered to reduce saturated fat and cholesterol levels, and to change the flavor a bit. But, this is not a health-food manual as I've sneaked in a few recipes for which my physician would never give his approval.

One final suggestion before I embark on descriptions of edible concoctions: put in a garden. You don't need 5 acres—my first garden was a raised bed only 8 by 12 feet. Two 12-foot and two 8-foot 2 by 12's and one 8-foot 2 by 4 (cut into 4 2-foot lenghts for corner posts) treated Douglas-fir boards plus 24 16-penny galvanized nails and 3° cubic yards of top soil are all you need to make a bed that will grow more vegetables than 1 person can eat.

From its humble beginnings, my garden has grown; it now consists of 3 8- by 12-foot and 2 8- by 16-foot beds. By double cropping (2 different crops on the same site during the same crop season) parts of these small plots, my spouse and I can produce and preserve enough vegetables for the 2 of us plus lots to give to friends, relatives, and charity. And, we can grow a much wider variety of vegetables than I could in my 1-bed garden. In many climates, with a little ingenuity, some fertilizer and water, and lots of labor you can grow vegetables of a quality never found in groceries. Not only are the fresh vegetables more tasty and nutritious, but your physical health will be improved by the labor required, your mental health inhanced by the diversion, and the produce will make a big dent in your food bill. And, best of all, it's a type of income that isn't taxable!

ACKNOWLEDGMENTS--I am especially grateful for the many hours that my bride spent at the computer helping me produce this book and equally endebted to her for consuming the products of my kitchen to which I added a bit too much of this or a bit too little of that. Thus, her critiques of my endeavors and suggestions for improvement are responsible for much of the quality of the recipes contained herein.

BREADS

Want to impress someone with your culinary skills? Making bread for them is the way to go. Some recipes are so easy that the only way to have a disaster is to omit an ingredient. Others are a bit more complex, but once you understand that yeast is a living organism thus can be killed easily and you learn the trick of kneading to activate the gluten in the flour you won't have any trouble.

Kneading bread dough can have great therapeutic effect. My new bride told me that she could always tell when I had had trouble with my department head the previous week by how loudly I made the breadboard squeak when I kneaded bread dough on Saturday morning. I knew that I always felt better after making bread each weekend, but I didn't realize that I was taking out my frustrations on the dough. Nevertheless, disagreements with my department head were responsible for some of the best loaves I ever made.

Not all breads have yeast and not all need to be kneaded. Some breads have sourdough as a special ingredient so are listed in the section with that title.

B.J.'s BREAD

2 tablespoons dry yeast (3 packages)	2 egg whites + ¼ cup egg substitute (Eggbeaters®)
1¼ cups 1% milk	9½ cups flour
1¼ cups water	1 tablespoon salt
½ cup canola oil	1 tablespoon canola oil
¾ cup sugar	Nonstick spray oil

In large mixing bowl, mix yeast, sugar, and water with mixer; let stand 5 minutes. Warm milk, oil, and salt in saucepan over medium heat until milk begins to froth; stir until salt is dissolved. Cool milk mixture until a drop on the back of the hand is barely warm, add to yeast mixture, and mix with mixer. Add eggs and mix. Add 4 cups flour to mixture and continue mixing with mixer until smooth. Add 4½ more cups of flour and mix with wooden spoon until single ball of dough forms. Turn out on well-floured breadboard and knead 100 times. Wash large mixing bowl, spread oil over entire inside of bowl, and return dough to bowl; cover with plastic wrap and let rise in warm place until dough doubles in size. Punch down, divide into thirds, and form into loaves. Spray inside of 3 bread pans with nonstick oil. Place loaves in pans, cover with plastic wrap, and let rise until almost double. Bake in 400°F oven for 30 minutes.

This is the first bread that I learned to make. Even though it is an excellent bread, I rarely make it now because I like the taste of sourdough breads better. The only failure that I ever had making this bread was when I dumped the scalded milk into the yeast mixture without cooling it first. Killed the yeast dead as a doorknob.

1 LOAF **B.J.'s BREAD** + 1 RECIPE FOR ROLLS

1⅓ tablespoons dry yeast
⅞ cup 1% milk
¾ cups water
⅓ cup canola oil
½ cup sugar

2 egg whites + ¼ cup egg substitute (Eggbeaters®)
6⅓ cups flour
⅔ tablespoon salt
⅔ tablespoon canola oil
Nonstick spray oil

Prepare the dough as for **B.J.'s BREAD**. Divide the dough into ⅔rd and ⅓rd portions. Use the ⅔rd portion for a loaf of bread and the ⅓rd portion for a batch of rolls.

ROLL OPTIONS

CLOVER-LEAF ROLLS

Tear off pieces of dough the size of a walnut and place 3 pieces in each section of muffin tin sprayed with nonstick oil. Cover with plastic wrap and let rise until rolls are ½–¾ inch above level of muffin tin. Bake in 400°F oven for 12–15 minutes. My family particularly likes these rolls at Thanksgiving and Christmas.

PARKER HOUSE ROLLS

Roll out dough with rolling pin until ⅜–½-inch thick. Cut with 2½-inch-diameter biscuit or cookie cutter. Fold each circle almost in half. Place in rectangular cake pan sprayed with nonstick oil. Reknead remaining dough briefly and roll out and cut another batch; repeat until all dough is used. Cover pan with plastic wrap and let rise until rolls are double. Bake in 400°F oven for 12–15 minutes.

CINNAMON ROLLS

Roll out dough with rolling pin until ⅜–½ inch thick. Spread with 3 tablespoons melted margarine, ¾ cup dark brown sugar, ½ cup dark raisins, and 1 tablespoon cinnamon. Carefully roll dough into "jelly-roll" then cut into 1-inch sections with sharp knife (or serrated bread knife). Turn each section on side in rectangular cake pan sprayed with nonstick oil. Cover pan with plastic wrap and let rolls rise until double. Bake in 400°F oven for 12–15 minutes.

PECAN ROLLS

Roll out dough with rolling pin until ⅜–½ inch thick. Spread with 3 tablespoons melted margarine, ¾ cup dark brown sugar, ¾ cup dark raisins, and ½ cup chopped pecans. Carefully roll dough into "jelly-roll" then cut into 1-inch sections with sharp knife (or serrated bread knife). Turn each section on side in rectangular cake pan sprayed with nonstick oil. Cover pan with plastic wrap and let rolls rise until double. Bake in 400°F oven for 12–15 minutes.

KNEADING DOUGH

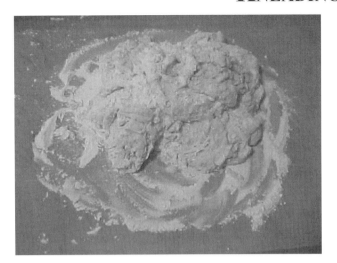

Step 1.— Dump dough on well-floured board.

Step 2.— Round dough into ball and fold into half.

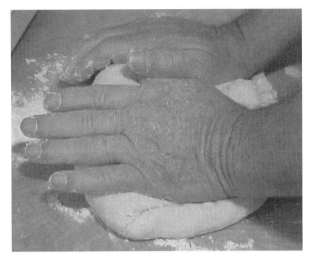

Step 3.—Compress folded ball and fold again. Repeat until dough becomes rubbery—about 50–100 times.

Step 4.— Add flour to board to prevent sticking.

Step 5.— Round dough into ball.

Step 6.— Place in oiled bowl and turn upside down. Cover bowl with plastic wrap or clean towel, place in warm area, and allow to rise.

SALT-RISING BREAD

2½ cups thinly sliced nonmealy potatoes
2 tablespoons yellow cornmeal
1 tablespoon salt
4 cups boiling water

On Thursday evening, peel potatoes and slice them paper-thin with a potato peeler. Place potatoes in deep dish, sprinkle with salt and cornmeal, add boiling water and cover (cover must not be air tight or mixture may explode). Keep in moderately warm place (65–68°F).

1 tablespoon baking soda
1½ teaspoons salt
5 cups flour

Early Saturday morning, pour liquid into large mixing bowl; discard potatoes. Mix salt, soda, and flour and add to liquid from potatoes. Beat with mixer. Set in warm place (72–80°F) until bubbles come to the top and the "sponge" has increased in size by ⅓ (2–5 hours depending on temperature).

1 cup milk
1 teaspoon sugar
1½ teaspoons margarine

Put the 3 ingredients in a saucepan, stir to dissolve sugar, and heat over medium heat until margarine is melted and milk is hot to touch—do not boil. Cool mixture by placing saucepan in cold water until a drop of milk feels barely warm to back of hand (105°F). Add to sponge and mix with mixer.

6+ cups flour
Nonstick spray oil

Add 4½–6 cups of flour to sponge and mix thoroughly with wooden spoon. Dump dough onto heavily floured breadboard and knead for 10 minutes, adding flour as needed to keep dough from sticking to breadboard. Dough should have a light and fluffy texture.

Shape into 3 loaves, place in loaf pans sprayed with nonstick oil. Spray top of loaves lightly with nonstick oil, cover with plastic wrap, and set in warm place until dough is almost doubled in bulk (about 1–1½ hours depending on temperature). Remove plastic wrap and bake at 350°F for 1 hour.

What a chore this bread is to make, 3 days, a dozen pans, and uncounted hours of checking on its progress. However, warm salt-rising bread, margarine, and strawberry jam, is an unbelieveable treat for a late Saturday afternoon snack! And, toasted for breakfast on Sunday morning this finely textured, but heavy and somewhat hard, bread is a second treat. Don't try, as my mother-in-law did even after being told not to, to use this for a sandwich bread.

Although this salt-rising bread is a much heavier bread, its nutty flavor reminds me of the bread that 50 years ago my step-father brought home every Tuesday—the day the local bakery produced the weekly batch of salt-rising bread. Save the remaining bread for future treats by double wrapping the remaining loaves in plastic bags (remove as much air as possible) and freeze for as long as 6 months.

Once, I tried adding 1 tablespoon dried yeast and ½ tablespoon sugar to the liquid (Saturday morning stage) in an attempt to produce a lighter bread. It did not affect the taste and it may have lightened the bread a little.

IRISH SODA BREAD

2 cups flour
1 cup cultured buttermilk (¼ cup dry buttermilk
   + 1 cup 1% milk can be substituted)
2 teaspoons baking powder
¼ teaspoon baking soda

3½ tablespoons sugar
2 teaspoons caraway seed
¾ cup raisins
2 teaspoons margarine
Nonstick spray oil

Mix dry ingredients (flour, baking powder, soda, 1½ tablespoons of sugar, caraway seed, and raisins). Make sure raisins are separated. Add buttermilk and stir until dough forms; if too dry to form a ball add a tablespoonful of buttermilk. Turn out dough onto well-floured breadboard and knead for 5—6 minutes. Add flour as needed to keep dough from sticking to board. Spray 8-inch cast-iron skillet with nonstick oil. Press dough into skillet; cut ¼-inch deep "+" on top of loaf. Bake 1 hour in 350°F oven. Remove from skillet, spread margarine over top of hot loaf, and sprinkle with remaining sugar. WARNING: Do not use skillet with plastic or wooden handle!

This quick bread is superb when slightly warm or cold. It is a great breakfast bread, especially with scrambled eggs or egg substitute. It is an excellent "tea" bread, too.

I gave this recipe to my son when he left for graduate school. He "wowed" all his friends and won the heart of the lady who was to become his bride by his skill at producing this easy-to-make, delicious bread—among other culinary skills that he learned from me!

IRISH SODA BREAD

RAISIN-OAT BREAD

1 tablespoon dry yeast	⅓ cup dark brown sugar
¼ cup warm water	2 teaspoons salt
2 cups 1% milk	4+ cups flour
3 tablespoons canola oil	1½ cups dark raisins
2 cups uncooked quick-cook rolled oats	Nonstick spray oil

Mix yeast and water in large mixing bowl with mixer for 2 minutes; let set for 5 minutes longer. Heat milk in saucepan over medium heat until milk is hot to touch with finger; dissolve salt in milk, then cool until a drop on back of hand is barely warm (105°F). Add milk, 2 tablespoons of oil, oats, sugar, and 1 cup of flour to yeast and mix with mixer at low speed. Add 2 more cups of flour and mix with wooden spoon until a ball of dough is formed. Turn out on well-floured breadboard and knead 100 times; add flour as needed to keep dough from sticking. Wash large mixing bowl and grease with remaining 1 tablespoon of oil; place dough in bowl, cover with plastic wrap, and let rise in warm place until dough is double in size. When double, turn out on breadboard, flatten dough into large circle and sprinkle with half of raisins. Fold dough in half, sprinkle with half of remaining raisins, and fold in half again. Repeat until all raisins are used. Knead dough to distribute raisins evenly throughout. With sharp knife cut dough into 2 equal pieces. Form each piece into loaf and place in bread pan sprayed with nonstick oil. Cover each loaf with plastic wrap and let rise in warm place until double. Bake in 350°F oven for 40 minutes. Remove from pans and cool on wire rack.

This is an excellent breakfast bread either warmed in microwave or toasted.

RAISIN-OAT BREAD

MULTI-BREAD

½ cup white cornmeal
½ cup brown sugar
1 tablespoon salt
2 cups boiling water
½ cup canola oil
¾ cup whole wheat flour

½ cup rye flour
4½–5½ cups unbleached white flour
2 tablespoons dry yeast
½ cup warm water
Nonstick spray oil

Pour first 5 ingredients into large mixing bowl, stir, and let cool. Dissolve yeast in warm water, then add to ingredients in mixing bowl. Add whole wheat and rye flours and enough white flour to make stiff dough. Knead 100 times, cover, and let rise until doubled. Punch down, divide in half, form into 2 loaves, and place in loaf pans sprayed with nonstick oil. Place in warm place and let rise until nearly doubled. Bake at 375° F for 35–40 minutes. Examine at 30 minutes; cover lightly with foil if browning too much.

GERIATRIC BREAD

2 tablespoons white cornmeal
2 tablespoons yellow cornmeal
1 tablespoon rolled barley
1 tablespoon rolled triticale
1 tablespoon rolled oats
1 tablespoon rolled rye
1 tablespoon sunflower seeds
1 tablespoon wheat bran
1 tablespoon oat bran
1 tablespoon wheat germ

¼ cup dark brown sugar
¼ cup canola oil
1 cup boiling water
¼ cup rye flour
¼ cup whole wheat flour
1 cup 60% gluten flour
1 cup white flour
1 tablespoon yeast
¼ cup warm water
Nonstick spray oil

In tiny mixing bowl add yeast to warm water, stir until dissolved and set aside until remaining ingredients are mixed. Place first 10 ingredients in blender and blend until seeds and rolled grains are flour-like. Add sugar, oil, and boiling water and mix thoroughly; set aside until cool. Pour yeast and moist ingredients into large mixing bowl and mix; add gluten flour and about half of white flour. Stir. Add remaining flour and continue stirring. Dough will be crumbly and a bit dry. Knead in mixing bowl until dough becomes a single lump. Place on dough board and knead 100 times. Place in mixing bowl lightly sprayed with nonstick oil, cover with plastic wrap, set in warm place, and let rise until doubled. Punch down, mold into loaf, place in loaf pan sprayed with non-stick oil, set in warm place, and let rise until doubled. Bake at 375°F for 40 minutes.

This is a heavy, gritty bread, but is guaranteed to replace a dose of laxative.

RYE ROUNDS

1 tablespoon dry yeast (2 packages)	1 teaspoon salt
1½ teaspoons sugar	1 teaspoon canola oil
2 cups warm water	1½ tablespoons caraway seed
2½ cups rye flour	3 tablespoons sesame seed
2½–3 cups white flour	Nonstick spray oil

In large mixing bowl, dissolve yeast in warm (105°F) water; add seeds, salt, sugar, and rye flour and beat with mixer until smooth. Add about 2½ cups of white flour and stir with wooden spoon. Turn out dough onto floured breadboard and knead (adding flour as needed) until dough is no longer sticky. Spray large mixing bowl with nonstick oil, add dough, and cover with plastic wrap. Place dough in warm place and let rise until double. Punch down dough and knead briefly. Spread 1 teaspoon canola oil on breadboard. Roll out chunks of dough to ¼-inch thickness. Cut with 3-inch-diameter cookie cutter. Place on cookie sheet sprayed with nonstick oil. Cover with plastic wrap and let rise until double. Prick each round 3 or 4 times with fork. Bake in 375°F oven for 30–35 minutes. For an extra hard bread that will last forever, reduce heat to 200°F and bake 30 minutes longer.

This is a great snacking bread. Munching on a couple of rye rounds makes the time go faster in a duck blind on a bluebird day or when it's your turn at the oars on a steelhead drift. Spread with "light" cream cheese, a rye round goes mighty good with a beer after work on a warm autumn afternoon. Even the lighter-baked rounds will keep for several months in the freezer.

SWEDISH RYE BREAD

1 tablespoon yeast	1 teaspoon ground cardamon seeds
1 tablespoon sugar	1 tablespoon caraway seeds
½ cup warm water	2 teaspoons monosodium glutamate
1 12-ounce can warm beer	2 tablespoons finely grated orange peel
¼ cup honey	2½ cups dark rye flour
2 tablespoons melted margarine	3 cups flour
2 teaspoons salt	Nonstick spray oil

Mix yeast, sugar, and warm water with mixer; let stand for 5 minutes. Grind spices with monosodium glutamate with mortar and pestle. Mix beer, spices, salt, honey, orange peel, and melted margarine, then add to yeast mixture. Mix flours in separate bowl, then add 3 cups to liquid and beat with mixer while scraping sides of bowl with rubber spatula. Cover mixture with plastic wrap and place in warm place for 50 minutes. Add half of remaining flour and stir until soft sticky dough forms. Place handful of remaining flour on board, turn out dough onto board, and kneed dough, adding remaining flour mixture as needed. When smooth, place ball of dough in bowl greased with margarine; be sure to grease top of ball of dough. Cover with plastic wrap and let rise in warm place for 50 minutes. Turn out dough on board and cut into half. Shape each half into ball, place on cookie sheet coated with non-stick spray oil, cover loosely with plastic wrap, and place in refrigerator for 3 hours. Remove from refrigerator and let stand at room temperature for 20 minutes. Bake at 375°F for 45 minutes; do not preheat oven.

XMAS ROLLS

1 tablespoon dry yeast
¼ cup warm water
1 cup milk
1 teaspoon salt
¼ cup sugar

¼ cup canola oil
1 egg white
2 tablespoons egg substitute (Eggbeaters®)
3+ cups flour
Nonstick spray oil

Heat milk in sauce pan over medium heat to scalding. Add salt, oil, and sugar, and cool to tepid (105°F). Dissolve yeast in warm water, let set for 5 minutes; add egg white and egg substitute to yeast and mix thoroughly. Combine mixtures; add half of flour and beat with mixer until smooth. Add remaining flour and mix with wooden spoon until soft dough forms. Turn out on well-floured board and knead for 5 minutes.

To bake immediately, place in well oiled mixing bowl, cover, and set in warm place; let rise until doubled. Form into rolls, set in or on pan sprayed with nonstick oil and let rise until double a second time. Bake in 400°F oven for 12–15 minutes.

To hold over night, cover with plastic wrap and refrigerate. Next day, set in warm place until double (2 hours or more). Form into rolls and bake as before.

Dough may be formed into clover-leaf or Parker House rolls; see recipe for **B.J.'s BREAD** (page 2) for descriptions. Recipe makes about 12 rolls or 6 rolls and 2 minature loaves (2- by 4-inch pans).

WHOLE WHEAT ROLLS

2 teaspoons dry yeast
⅓ cup warm water
⅓ cup hot water
2 tablespoons honey
¼ cup canola oil

½ teaspoon salt
2 tablespoons egg substitute (Eggbeaters®)
2+ cups whole wheat flour
Nonstick spray oil

Mix yeast with warm (105°F) water and let set 5 minutes. Mix honey, oil, and salt with hot water; stir until honey is dissolved completely, then cool to body temperature. Add egg substitute and yeast mixture and stir. Add 2 cups flour and stir until mixture forms a ball of dough—add flour a tablespoon at a time if necessary to form ball.

Dough may be formed into rolls immediately, but is a bit sticky to work with. If cooled in refrigerator for 1–2 hours, dough is easier to handle.

Spray cups in muffin tin with nonstick oil. Form dough into balls 1 inch in diameter. Place 3 balls per muffin cup. Cover with plastic wrap and place in warm place to rise. When slightly more than doubled, bake in oven preheated to 425°F for 10–12 minutes. Makes about a dozen rolls.

To provide a "warm place" for this and other yeast doughs to rise, place in the oven preheated to the lowest temperature (mine is 100°F) for 2 minutes. Place a teakettle full of boiling water in the bottom of the oven. Temperature in oven should remain at near optimum for yeast to rise for 1–1½ hours.

CORNBREAD

1 cup yellow cornmeal
1 cup cultured buttermilk (¼ cup powdered buttermilk + 1 cup 1% milk may be substituted for cultured
    buttermilk)
½ teaspoon salt
½ teaspoon baking soda
1 egg white
2 tablespoons egg substitute (Eggbeaters®)
2 tablespoons canola oil

Preheat oven to 450°F. Pour oil in 8-inch cast-iron skillet and heat over medium burner. Mix dry ingredients. Add egg and buttermilk and mix thoroughly with wisk. When oil just commences to smoke, remove skillet from heat and rotate to coat sides of skillet. Be sure to handle skillet with hot pad or cooking glove. Pour hot oil into batter and mix thoroughly with wisk. Immediately pour batter back into skillet; use rubber spatula to remove all of batter. Bake 20 minutes at 450°F. Dump out of skillet onto breadboard and cut into 6 wedges; split wedges and insert margarine. This is an excellent accompaniment for many soups and fish dishes. Freeze left-over wedges for use in turkey dressing.

Use larger skillet if you like thinner, crispy cornbread. To make cornbread sticks, spray cast-iron form with nonstick oil and heat in oven to 450°F before pouring in batter. WARNING: Do not use skillet with plastic or wooden handle!

BREAD CUBES, BREAD CRUMBS, AND CROUTONS

Several gallon-size plastic bags full of stale bread, rolls, or biscuits

Keep a plastic bag in the freezer compartment of the refrigerator for heels and left-over bread. As the bread becomes stale, but before it molds, place it in the bag. When the bag fills, move it to the freezer. When several bags accumulate, cut the bread into cubes, spread on cookie sheets, and allow them to become thoroughly dried. Sheets containing bread cubes may be placed in the oven when it is turned off after cooking a dish therein, or they can be placed in front of heating ducts or small electric fan. The only restrictions are that the bread cubes be dried in a vermin-, dust-, and springer spaniel-free place while drying.

For crumbs, cut cubes ¾–1 inch, for bread dressings, about ½-inch cubes seem best, and for croutons for salads make them ¼–⅜ inches. To make crumbs, use the blender. For salad croutons, spray cubes with olive or grape-seed oil, add toasted sesame seeds, black pepper, and paprika. Undried cubes for croutons may be toasted in oven set on broil. Watch toasting croutons constantly, when they begin to brown, remove from oven, stir and replace in oven. Repeat as necessary to obtain desired crispness and color. Store croutons and crumbs in the freezer—a 3-pound coffee can makes an easy-to-handle container.

Bread crumbs made with 50% or more whole wheat, rye, or multi-grain breads are best. They add flavor to meat loaves, meat balls, and fried eggplant and zucchini.

1976-BICENTENNIAL TURKEY DRESSING

5 cups dried bread cubes (at least half should be dark breads)
1 cup left-over corn bread, cubed
¾ cup chopped onion
¾ cup chopped celery (include some tender leaves)
¾ cup chopped mushrooms
2 cloves garlic
¼ cup chopped green pepper
2 tablespoons canola oil
1 teaspoon poultry seasoning
1 teaspoons sage
1 teaspoon salt
⅛ teaspoon freshly ground black pepper
1 bay leaf
Small sprig fresh rosemary
2 egg whites
¼ cup egg substitute (Eggbeaters®)
2–3 cups liquid (broth or roast-turkey drippings with fat removed; may be extended with as much as ½
    cup 1% milk)
Nonstick spray oil

Chop onions, celery, garlic, mushrooms, green pepper, rosemary, and bay leaf; saute in oil until onion is limp and translucent. Discard bay leaf and rosemary. Place bread cubes, remaining spices, and eggs in large mixing bowl; mix thoroughly. Add sauted vegetables and ⅓ of liquid at a time. Stir until all material is wetted thoroughly. Pour into 1¾-quart Corningware baking dish sprayed with nonstick oil. Use rubber spatula to remove material from sides of baking dish and to shape dressing into loaf. Bake for 45 minutes at 350°F. It is strongly recommended that this method of baking dressing be used rather than stuffing body cavity of turkey with dressing.

See recipe for **TURKEY GIBLET GRAVY** (page 72) for instructions regarding production of broth.

I first made this recipe the second time that I roasted a turkey for Thanksgiving. My first try, a year earlier, was reasonably tasty, but without the vegetables (onion, green pepper, mushrooms, celery, and garlic) it was a bit pasty. I decided, upon my second try, to overcome the heavy texture by adding whatever vegetables I had in the refrigerator. A dish of this dressing has accompanied the roast turkey for most Christmas and Thanksgiving dinners since.

12-CUP MUFFIN TIN

6-CUP MUFFIN TIN WITH PAPERS

MUFFINS

Six months or so after I became chief cook (and commonly bottle washer, too), I decided to make a complete inventory of various paraphenalia in the kitchen cabinets. In digging through a corner cabinet below the counter, I encountered 2 muffin tins, a 6-holer and a 12-holer. And, on another shelf above the counter, I found a package of paper muffin cups. Wow! Now I can make cup cakes! I mixed a chocolate cake mix according to instructions on the package, put a paper muffin cup into each hole in the muffin tins, added about an inch of cake mix, and baked the lot. It is difficult to list my mistakes in order either of occurrence or seriousness. I didn't spray the cups with nonstick oil, so the cake stuck to the cups. I baked the cup cakes the same length of time recommended for a 1-pan cake, so the cakes were beyond dry. And, I didn't fill the cups nearly full enough, so the cake in 1 cup did not constitute a full serving. For dessert during the following couple of days, my son and I chewed on crispy chocolate cake scraped from 2 or 3 of the paper cups. Alas, it is our mistakes from which we learn! My subsequent prepared-cake-mix cup cakes improved in esthetics, texture, and sapidity.

Although my son and I enjoyed the cup cakes, the appelation "muffin tin" brought to mind the odor and taste of freshly baked bran muffins with lots of raisins. I found a couple of recipes for bran muffins in the cook book my friend gave me and tried them. Although a bit pasty, they were reasonably palatable. I wanted more, so I began to experiment—adding some of this and reducing or eliminating some of that. My favorite muffin recipes follow.

SORGHUM-BRAN MUFFINS

1 cup flour
½ teaspoon salt
1 teaspoon soda
1 cup wheat bran
½ cup bran cereal
½ cup dark raisins
1 egg white
¼ cup egg substitute (Eggbeaters®)
¼ cup brown sugar
¼ cup sorghum molasses

¾ cup buttermilk
1½ tablespoons canola oil
½ cup acidophilous yogurt
1 teaspoon cinnamon
¼ teaspoon nutmeg
¼ teaspoon mace
¼ teaspoon allspice
¼ teaspoon cloves
Nonstick spray oil

Mix dry ingedients; separate raisins and add to dry ingredients, mix thoroughly. Mix liquid ingredients in separate bowl; make sure sorghum is dissolved. Add liquids to dry ingredients and mix thoroughly. Place paper cups in muffin tin, spray with nonstick spray oil, fill cups ¾th's full with muffin dough, and bake at 425°F for 25 minutes.

REFRIGERATOR BRAN MUFFINS

¼ cup dark brown sugar
¼ cup white sugar
¼ cup canola oil
2 tablespoons wheat germ
½ cup wheat-flakes breakfast cereal
1 cup raisins
¾ tablespoon baking soda
¼ tablespoon salt
2 egg whites
1¼ cups flour

1 cup bran flakes (not cereal, but true wheat bran)
1¼ cups cultured buttermilk
2 teaspoons cinnamon
¼ teaspoon nutmeg
1 teaspoon allspice
½ teaspoon cloves
½ teaspoon mace
Nonstick spray oil
Paper muffin cups

Mix sugars, oil, egg whites, and buttermilk in large mixing bowl until homogenized. In separate mixing bowl blend together remaining dry ingredients, including raisins; add to wet ingredients and mix thoroughly. Place paper muffin cup in each space in muffin tin. Spray inside of paper cup lightly with nonstick spay oil. With 2 spoons (1 large, 1small) place dough into muffin cups; fill each cup with what appears to be enough to fill it ⅔rd's full, but don't try to spread the dough evenly. Bake at 400°F for 23 minutes. Muffins are better if dough is refrigerated for at least 3 days before using. Dough, covered in a refrigerator, will keep for about 6 weeks; it improves with age.

REFRIGERATOR OAT-BRAN MUFFINS

One Sunday morning, I arose early and decided to give my new bride a treat by serving hot bran muffins. With half the ingredients mixed, I discovered that my supply of bran flakes was only ½ cup. I simply substituted ½ cup uncooked quick-cook rolled oats. The revised recipe instantly became a new culinary delight in our household. So, don't wait until your supply of bran flakes is less than the 1 cup called for in the previous recipe to substitute quick-cook oats for part of them. Keep everything else the same, including cooking temperature and time.

TRAVELING OAT-BRAN MUFFINS

When traveling cross-country by automobile, my spouse and I usually have breakfast consisting of a muffin, the whites of a couple of **HARD-BOILED EGGS** (page 103), a piece of reduced-fat Farmers, Havarti, Jack, or Mozzarella cheese, a glass of orange juice, and a cup of tea. A dozen baked muffins kept in an ice chest is enough for the 6-day trip to the East Coast. But, what about the return trip? I modified the previous recipe a bit, put the dry ingredients in a plastic bag, and before leaving for home talked a friend or relative into loaning us use of an oven.

⅓ cup dark brown sugar
¼ cup white sugar
¼ cup wheat germ
¼ cup oat bran
½ cup wheat-flakes breakfast cereal (crushed)
4 teaspoons powdered egg whites
1¼ cups flour
1 cup raisins
¾ tablespoon baking soda

½ cup bran flakes (not cereal, but true wheat bran)
½ cup quick-cook rolled oats
¼ cup + 1 tablespoon powdered buttermilk
2 teaspoons cinnamon
¼ teaspoon nutmeg
¼ tablespoon salt
1 teaspoon allspice
½ teaspoon cloves
½ teaspoon mace

Mix thoroughly and store in zip-lock bag. When ready to use, add:

1¾ cups cold water (or 1% milk)
¼ cup canola oil

Mix thoroughly. Also, a muffin tin, nonstick spray oil, and paper muffin cups will be needed. Better take them with you in the event the friend or relative that loans you use of an oven doesn't have them. Keep everything else the same, including cooking temperature and time.

APPLE-CAKE MUFFINS

To 1 recipe of **FRESH APPLE CAKE** (page 122) add 1 cup quick-cook rolled oats, ¼ teaspoon baking powder, and ¼ cup flour. Spray paper cup-cake cups with nonstick spray oil. Spoon cups level full with batter. Bake 30 minutes at 350°F. Makes about 15 muffins. Freeze excess muffins, but not the dough.

SOURDOUGH APPLE-BUCKWHEAT PANCAKES—page 18

SOURDOUGH

Sourdough cookery adds a new dimension to your culinary skills. Requirements include a ½-gallon stoneware jar with stoneware lid, a sourdough starter, and a back corner of the refrigerator. If no acquaintance maintains a sourdough starter, you commonly can find starters in garden shops, nutrition centers, or health-food stores. Or, as a last resort, you can use acidophilous yogurt. My starter came from a friend who got it from an old professor in Canada who I think obtained it from someone who had prospected during the Klondike Gold Rush in Yukon Territory. Interestingly, I was able to give a start back to my friend when her sourdough died and she, in turn, gave some to the old professor when he lost his sourdough. So, the starter made full circle.

Commence making the sourdough by mixing 2 cups of flour, 2 cups of milk (this is a great way to make use of sour milk), ½ cup sugar, and ½–1 cup starter (or ¼ cup acidophilous yogurt). Stir with wire whisk until batter is smooth. Cover (but DO NOT SEAL) and place in refrigerator for 5–7 days. Stir well with whisk before using. Retain at least 1 cup of each batch for starter.

To feed dough add 1 cup flour, 1 cup milk, and ¼ cup sugar or more of the 3 components in that ratio. Adjust sourdough to desired consistency when feeding by adding or subtracting 1–2 tablespoons of milk. Do not overfeed as sourdough will overflow jar and make a mess of your refrigerator.

Sourdough makes unbelieveably light pancakes and waffles, "down-home" type biscuits, and a French bread that will make your mouth water when you take it from the oven. See the recipes that follow.

GOLD-FIELD SOURDOUGH PANCAKES

1 cup sourdough starter
1 tablespoon sugar
¼ teaspoon salt
½ teaspoon baking soda

1 egg white + ¼ cup egg substitute (Eggbeaters®)
1½ tablespoons canola oil
1 tablespoon water
Nonstick spray oil

Turn heat on medium under griddle. Mix sourdough, sugar, salt, egg, and oil; beat until smooth. In separate container (I use ¼-cup measure) mix soda and water. When griddle is hot, FOLD soda into batter gently (I use an ice tea spoon). DO NOT BEAT! When batter fills with bubbles (about 30 seconds) it is ready to bake. Spray griddle with nonstick oil, wait until it turns light brown; pour on ½+ cup per pancake. Turn cakes when bubbles on surface of cakes do not close. Makes 4 6–7-inch-diameter cakes.

SOURDOUGH BUCKWHEAT PANCAKES

Add 2 tablespoons buckwheat flour and 1 tablespoon milk to basic sourdough pancake recipe.

SOURDOUGH APPLE-BUCKWHEAT PANCAKES

Grate 1 medium apple into buckwheat option and mix thoroughly before adding soda-water mixture. I like Red Rome or Granny Smith apples. This, by far, is the best pancake recipe that I've developed.

SOURDOUGH OATBRAN PANCAKES

Add 2 tablespoons oatbran and 1 tablespoon milk to basic sourdough pancake recipe. Let stand 4–5 minutes before adding soda.

SOURDOUGH RICE-FLOUR PANCAKES

Add 2 tablespoons brown rice flour and 1 tablespoon milk to basic sourdough recipe. Rice flour makes a lacy and crispy surface on cakes.

SOURDOUGH WAFFLES

1 cup flour (unsifted)
1 teaspoon baking powder
½ teaspoon soda
¼ teaspoon salt
3 tablespoons canola oil

1 cup sourdough
2 egg whites + ½ cup egg substitute (Eggbeaters®)
½–¾ cup milk (sufficient to make moderately thin dough)
Nonstick spray oil

Begin to heat waffle iron; if automatic iron, continue to heat for 4–5 minutes after iron signals that it is hot enough to bake waffles. Mix flour, baking powder, soda, and salt, add sourdough, oil, eggs, and ½ cup milk. Beat until smooth. Add additional milk if necessary to make moderately thin dough. Spray iron with nonstick spray oil. Add about ¾ cup dough to iron and cook until iron signals that waffle is cooked. Spray iron with nonstick oil before cooking each waffle. Makes 4 waffles.

SOURDOUGH OATBRAN WAFFLES

For an interesting change in texture and flavor add ¼ cup oatbran and enough extra milk to adjust batter to the same consistency.

SOURDOUGH CHERRY-CHOCOLATE CAKE

1 pint (202 can) tart pie cherries (not cherry-pie mix)
1 cup flour
½ cup sourdough
¼ cup milk

Drain liquid from cherries into mixing bowl (refrigerate cherries) and add enough milk to make 1 cup. Add sourdough and flour, mix thoroughly, cover mixing bowl with cloth or plastic wrap and set in warm place overnight.

1 cup pecans
½ cup flour
½ cup canola oil
1½ cups sugar
½ cup powdered cocoa
½+ cup semisweet chocolate chips
4 egg whites or 2 egg whites + ¼ cup egg substitute (Eggbeaters®)
½ teaspoon cinnamon
½ teaspoon nutmeg
½ teaspoon mace
2 teaspoons baking soda
Nonstick spray oil
Powdered sugar

Chop nuts. Cream together oil and sugar with mixer; add eggs and continue to mix. Add spices, cocoa, flour, and soda and continue mixing. Add starter and beat until smooth; add cherries, chocolate chips, and nuts.

Spray 9- by 13-inch cake pan with nonstick oil. Pour in batter and spread evenly. Bake in oven at 350°F for 45 minutes, until cakes pulls from sides of pan. Stick cake with a toothpick—if it comes out covered with dough bake it another 5 minutes and test it again. Cool on rack; refrigerate. Rewarm individual pieces in microwave (½–¾ minute per serving) and dust with powdered sugar just before serving if desired. Cake improves with age and is far superior when eaten warmed to melt the chocolate chips. If you are a chocolate lover, you must try this one.

For a really luscious cake substitute broken-up Hershey's Special Dark Chocolate® bars for the semisweet chocolate chips.

**SOURDOUGH CHERRY-CHOCOLATE
CAKE**

SOURDOUGH FRENCH BREAD

2 tablespoons (or 3 packages) dry yeast
1 cup warm water (barely warm to the back of your hand; too hot and you will kill the yeast)
2 tablespoons sugar
4 cups sourdough
½ tablespoon salt
3 tablespoons canola oil
2 egg whites
7–8 cups flour
1–2 tablespoons yellow cornmeal
Nonstick spray oil

In large mixing bowl, mix yeast, water, and sugar with mixer; add sourdough and continue mixing until smooth. Remove from mixer and set aside for 4–5 minutes. In mean time, beat egg whites until stiff. Add beaten egg whites to sourdough mixture and beat with mixer until egg whites are completely mixed into sourdough. Add salt, oil, and 3 cups of flour 1 cup at a time. With rubber spatula, wipe partly mixed flour into mixture. Remove from mixer. Add 3–3½ cups flour and stir with long-handled wooden spoon until flour is completely mixed into dough. Spread ½ cup flour on bread board and pour dough on top of it. Rub a few pinches of flour inside of bowl to remove all of dough. Knead dough vigorously for 10 minutes, adding flour as needed to keep dough from sticking to board.

Wash large mixing bowl while dough rests on bread board. Spread 1 tablespoon of canola oil on inside of bowl. Return dough to bowl, cover with plastic wrap, and set in warm place to rise. (I place loaves in oven that has been turned on for 1 minute only.) When dough doubles in size, punch down, and return it to bread board. Flatten into a circle and cut into quarters. Spray 2 double French-bread loaf pans with nonstick oil and sprinkle with cornmeal. Roll and twist each quarter of dough into elongated loaf to fit French-bread loaf pans. Leave about 1½ inches free of dough at each end of pans. Cover loaves with plastic wrap. Place in warm place and let rise. When loaves double in size, score each loaf diagonally across the top about ⅛ inch deep at 2-inch intervals with a clean razor blade. Spray or brush lightly with water. Heat oven to 425°F; place loaves in oven for 10 minutes, then reduce heat to 325°F and bake for another 40 minutes. Spray or brush loaves lightly with water at 10-minute intervals. When done, slide loaves onto rack to cool.

This is an unbelieveably enticing bread; you won't be able to keep from slicing off a chunk and spreading it with margarine while it is still warm.

SOURDOUGH APRICOT-RAISIN BREAD

1 cup sourdough
1 cup flour
3 tablespoons canola oil
½ cup dark brown sugar
¾ cup dark raisins
½ cup white sugar
¼ teaspoon baking soda

2 egg whites or 1 egg white + 2 tablespoons
    egg substitute (Eggbeaters®)
1 teaspoon baking powder
½ teaspoon salt
¾ cup chopped pecans
¾ cup dried apricots (finely chopped)
Nonstick spray oil

Spray loaf pan with nonstick oil. Mix egg, sugar, and oil in mixer; add sourdough mixture and continue to mix. Mix dry ingredients in another bowl including nuts and fruit. Add dry ingredients to sourdough mixture and mix 2 minutes. Pour batter in pan; bake in oven at 350°F for 1 hour. Cool on rack. Keeps 6 weeks or more in refrigerator. Great sliced, toasted, and spread with a bit of margarine.

SOURDOUGH BAKING POWDER BISCUITS

1 cup sourdough
1 cup flour
3 tablespoons canola oil
2 teaspoons baking powder

½ teaspoon baking soda
½ teaspoon salt
Nonstick spray oil

Mix dry ingredients in medium mixing bowl; add oil and sourdough. Mix with fork until dough forms a single ball. Add 1–2 tablespoons flour to cause biscuit dough to form ball. Kneed dough in hands for 10 seconds. Spread 2 tablespoons flour on bread board; add dough and flatten with hand. Roll with rolling pin until ⅜–½ inch thick. Cut with biscuit cutter (or if you were poor as I was, use a small tin can from which both ends have been removed). Place biscuits on cookie sheet sprayed with nonstick oil. Roll remaining dough into another ball and repeat until all is used. Make sure that the top of each biscuit has a little unwetted flour on its top. Let biscuits stand in a warm place for about 10 minutes. Bake in oven at 425°F for 10–12 minutes. Makes about a dozen 2½-inch biscuits. (My son calls these "dusty" biscuits because of the flour that I leave on top.)

**SOURDOUGH BAKING POWDER
BISCUITS**

SOURDOUGH SCONES

Replace 1 cup of flour with ½ cup quick-cook rolled oats plus ⅓ cup flour in **SOURDOUGH BAKING POWDER BISCUIT** (page 21) recipe. Process dough as before except cut into 6 equal parts. Roll each piece of dough into a ball, then flatten between the hands until the scone is about 2½–3 inches in diameter. Alternatively, roll dough into 6–7 inch circle and cut into 6 wedge-shaped pieces. Bake same as biscuits.

SOURDOUGH ENGLISH MUFFINS

½ cup warm water
1 tablespoon dry yeast
2 teaspoons sugar
1 teaspoon salt
½ cup milk
3 tablespoons canola oil

4 teaspoons sugar
1 cup sourdough
3+ cups flour
½ cup white cornmeal
Nonstick spray oil

Combine first 3 ingredients in large mixing bowl, mix with mixer, and let stand 5–10 minutes. Mix next 4 ingredients in sauce pan and scald; add cold sourdough, mix, and cool to tepid. Add ingredients in sauce pan to those in large mixing bowl. Add 2 cups flour and mix with mixer. Remove from mixer and mix in 1 cup flour. Turn out on floured board and knead 2 minutes. Dough is extremely sticky, so requires flour to avoid sticking to board and fingers. Wash mixing bowl, oil lightly, and return kneaded dough to bowl. Place bowl in warm place for 45 minutes or until dough is doubled. Return dough to floured board and press with hand until about ¼ inch thick. Cut with 3-inch-diameter cookie cutter. Place dough circles 1 inch apart on cookie sheet that has been sprayed with nonstick oil and sprinkled with cornmeal. Dust dough circles with a little flour and cover with plastic wrap. Let rise in warm place 30–40 minutes.

Heat griddle sprayed with nonstick oil at medium heat until oil browns. Transfer dough circles to griddle with pancake turner. Dip pancake turner into flour before handling dough circle to avoid sticking. Bake until brown (about 3–4 minutes), turn and brown second side. Set aside to cool.

CEREALS

As a child, I was served a variety of cereals, both hot and cold. I never cared much for any of them. Most of the cold cereals became soggy before I could completely ingest them and most of the hot ones were too pasty. Perhaps the latter problem could be overcome by appropriate moist-dry component ratios, but I was never moved to experiment. As sort of a lark 1 day, I purchased small amounts of several rolled grains, mixed the lot, and cooked an appropriate amount. Eureka! A cooked cereal that wasn't pasty!

GERIATIC CEREAL

1 cup old-fashoned rolled oats
1 cup rolled barley
1 cup rolled triticale
1 cup rolled rye flakes

Mix thoroughly and store in air-tight container in freezer. To prepare, bring 1½ cups water to boil over high heat, add ½ teaspoon salt and ⅔ cup (tightly packed) cereal mixture. Reduce heat to medium-low, partially cover pan, and cook, stirring occasionally, for about 15 minutes until all water is absorbed. Serve with sugar or milk and sugar. Makes 2 large servings.

This cereal not only contains considerable fiber, but has an excellent flavor and texture. It lacks the pasty texture of rolled oats.

CREAM OF RICE

¼ cup cream of rice cereal
1½ cups water
½ teaspoon salt
2 teaspoons margarine

Bring salted water to boil over high heat. Turn off heat and add cream of rice cereal, stirring constantly. Stir for 1 minute, remove from heat, and cover for 1 minute. Add 1 teaspoon margarine to each of the 2 servings. Plain this is good with egg-substitute omelet for breakfast. Add a few small pieces of reduced-fat Havarti cheese and mix well for a great winter-evening snack.

FRIED MUSH

½ cup white cornmeal
1¾ cups water
½ teaspoon salt

½ cup cold water
Nonstick spray oil

Mix cold water, salt, and cornmeal. Heat remaining water to boiling. Add cornmeal-water mix. Stir constantly over moderate heat—adjust heat so that cornmeal does not spatter out of pan. Cook 5–8 minutes until mush is thick. Pour into 3- by 6-inch loaf pan sprayed with nonstick oil. Cool in refrigerator over night.

Turn out "loaf" of mush onto wax paper. Slice about ½-inch thick with thin knife (ham slicer or bread knife). Lay slices on heavily floured wax paper; sprinkle with flour or turn with spatula and coat both sides with flour. Saute in canola or grapeseed oil over medium high burner until brown and crisp on both sides. Serve for breakfast with eggs (or egg substitute) and strawberry jam or sorghum molasses.

This is another 1 of those dishes that I remember from my Depression-era childhood. I commonly was served the cooked cornmeal while still hot as an accompaniment to egg dishes for breakfast 1 day and the cold and congealed left-overs sauted in lard the next. Despite eliminating the saturated fat in the lard, the considerable amount of oil absorbed by the cooking cornmeal slices make this a dish that probably should be consumed infrequently.

GENESE'S MICROWAVED GRITS

1¾ quart casserole
⅓ cup Quick grits
1 cup water
⅓ teaspoon salt
1 tablespoon margarine

⅓ cup 1% milk
1 egg white
⅓ cup egg substitute (Eggbeaters®)
⅓ cup grated Tillamook® cheddar cheese

In covered casserole microwave on high first 4 ingredients for 5 minutes. Stir and continue to microwave for 2 minutes. Add margarine, milk, and eggs. Microwave for 4 minutes. Stir and microwave for 4 minutes more. Add cheese, stir, and let stand for 1–2 minutes to allow cheese to melt. Serves 2.

SUGGESTED VARIATIONS: Add green pepper, onion, ham, and/or garlic when milk is added. I prefeer 1 slice of 97% fat-free sandwich ham chopped into ¼-inch squares added with the milk and eggs.

My bride hated grits! I tried several recipes — she turned up her nose at all of them. So, I threw out my box of grits and resigned myself to never again enjoy one of my favorite breakfast dishes. Then, on a trip east, we stayed overnight with friends in northern Illinois. Our friends fed us this dish for breakfast. About 100 miles down the road I got the courage to ask my bride what she thought of breakfast. She loved it; I was back in the grits business! I must admit that I've modified the recipe our friends gave us to reduce fat and cholesterol.

STARCHES

Starches are the "gasoline" that fuel our "internal combustion" engines. Athletes reduce starches in their diet for a couple of days, then pack in the starches for a couple of days before competitive events. This loads their muscle cells with carbohydrates so they have greater endurance. Even those of us who are not competitive athletes still need starches provided by rice, potatoes, grains, pastas, and a variety of other foods.

Many of the starch foods are relatively easy to cook, but to the neophyte as I was, proper times and temperatures are legitimate concerns. I recall my first attempt at cooking rice; the grain had been poured into a plastic container from the package in which it was purchased. So, off to the grocery I went to purchase another package of rice to obtain instructions for cooking the stuff.

STEAMED RICE

1 cup long-grain converted rice
2½ cups water
1 teaspoon salt

Bring salted water to boil in covered sauce pan. Add rice, cover, and reduce heat to medium. Cook about 24–25 minutes, or until all water is absorbed.

RICE PILAF

1 cup long-grain white rice
¼ cup wild rice
2¾ cups water
½ tablespoon salt

10 medium mushrooms
1 small onion
1 tablespoon chopped parsley
1 tablespoon canola oil

Bring salted water to boil in 2-quart sauce pan. Add rices, reduce heat to medium-low and cook until all water is absorbed (about 24–25 minutes). Heat oil in large skillet, add finely chopped mushrooms and onion and saute until onion is limp and translucent. Turn off heat, add to cooked rice, and stir in parsley. Serve immediately. This is an excellent dish with beef, chicken, or turkey.

RICE PILAF, TOO

1 cup long-grain white rice
2½ cups water
1 cup chicken broth
1½ teaspoons chicken bouillon
1 small onion finely chopped

2 cloves garlic finely chopped
½ green pepper finely chopped
4 medium mushrooms finely chopped
1 tablespoon canola oil

Place oil in 2-quart sauce pan and heat over medium heat; add vegetables and saute until onion is limp and translucent. Add water, broth, and bouillon, and bring to a boil. Add rice, lower heat to medium-low, and cook for 24–25 minutes or until all water is absorbed. Serve immediately.

FRIED RICE

½ recipe left-over **STEAMED RICE** (page 25)
1 small onion (1½–2 inches in diameter)
½ green pepper

1–2 tablespoon sesame oil
1 tablespoon soy sauce
Nonstick spray oil

Chop onion and pepper finely. Heat ½ tablespoon sesame oil in wok sprayed with nonstick oil. Saute onion and pepper until onion becomes translucent. Add rice and begin to stirfry, breaking clumps of rice. Sprinkle with soy sauce and additional sesame oil. Continue to stirfry until rice is completely coated with oil and hot through. Serve with grilled snapper or broiled chicken.

CORN ON THE COB

4 ears sweet corn
1 teaspoon salt
1½ quarts of water

Fill small stock pot half full of water. Add salt and bring to boil. Add cleaned and clipped ears of sweet corn. Bring to boiling, reduce heat, and simmer for 10 minutes. To cook frozen ears of corn do not thaw, but drop frozen ears into boiling water, bring to boiling, reduce heat, and simmer for 10 minutes.

The key to good corn on the cob is in the selection of corn. Choose ears that have moderate sized grains that are not excessively starchy. Sugars are converted to starch in corn between the time the corn is picked and the time that it is cooked. Therefore, pick ears that have green and succulent husks and on which the silks are not brown and dry. Refrigerate corn after purchase to retard conversion of sugars to starch. And, for the best corn of all—grow your own and pick it 10 minutes before you drop it into boiling water.

To clean corn properly, remove husks, clip about ½–¾ inch from silk end of ear, and remove silks under running water by scrubbing gently with plastic vegetable brush. Brush only in direction of long axis of ear.

OVEN FRENCH FRIES

2 large Kennabec potatoes
2–3 tablespoons canola oil

Peel potatoes and cut them into long narrow stips about ⅜ inch by ⅜ inch by as long as the potato. Sprinkle with oil and mix until all potatoes are evenly coated with oil. Bake in 550°F oven for 25–30 minutes until golden brown; stir at about 5-minute intervals.

These potatoes aren't quite the same as those deep fried in hot fat, but they certainly have many fewer calories and no cholesterol. They are surprisingly good however.

SCALLOPED POTATOES

6–7 2½–3-inch-diameter Kennebec potatoes
¼ cup finely chopped onion
2 tablespoons canola oil
¼ cup flour
½ tablespoon salt
⅛ teaspoon pepper
2½ cups 1% milk
¼ cup Parmesan cheese
Nonstick spray oil

Peel potatoes and slice ⅛ inch thick. Spray 1¾-quart Corningware casserole with nonstick oil; arrange potatoes in alternate layers with chopped onion. Sprinkle layers with a little salt.

In sauce pan, heat oil over medium heat; add flour and stir. Add milk, salt, pepper, and cheese. Stir with whisk over medium-high heat until sauce thickens. When thick and bubbly, pour over potatoes—use knife to open channels permiting sauce to run alongside and in crevices between pieces of potato. Cover with glass lid and bake for 1 hour at 350°F; remove cover and bake for 30 minutes more.

CREAMED NEW POTATOES

10 small new Kennebec potatoes about 1–1½ inches in diameter
1 cup 1% milk
1 teaspoon margarine
3 tablespoons flour
½ teaspoon salt
dash freshly ground black pepper
2 tablespoons Parmesan cheese

Scrub potatoes with plastic vegetable brush until peel is entirely removed. Place potatoes in steamer rack over ½-inch water in deep sauce pan. Bring to boiling, then reduce heat to medium and cook until potatoes can be penetrated easily with fork—about 20 minutes. Remove steamer rack with potatoes. Dissolve flour in cold milk and add to ½ cup of the water in bottom of sauce pan. Add margarine, salt, pepper, and Parmesan cheese. Cook on medium-high burner stirring constantly until thick and bubbly. Pour potatoes from steamer rack into sauce, stir, and serve.

My mother commonly added half a cup or so of partially cooked English peas to the sauce while it was cooking. The small green spheres between the large white spheres made an attractive and tasty dish.

This is a dish for which you likely will need to grow your own potatoes as I have rarely seen small new potatoes in a grocery store. These are the ones that can be pilfered from the growing potato plants beginning in early July. Simply press the fingers into the soft soil until a small potato is encountered, then dig it out; the plants aren't hurt and will grow other tubers. Growing potatoes is a rather easy chore in many climates and the harvests can be bountiful. My spouse and I grow Kennebec potatoes; the growing tubers of this variety have a habit of protruding onto the surface and becoming green. The green of potatoes is toxic and should never be consumed, so those potatoes must be discarded. My spouse complained to the local extension gardener about the greening problem and was told to add compost to the surface of the ground. It helped, but did not eliminate the problem. She returned to complain to the extension gardner. He asked how big her potato patch was and she responded "Eight by eight feet." He asked how many potatoes she harvested from her patch and she told him "About 2½ bushels of good ones." He produced a hand calculator and quickly calculated that we were obtaining the equivalent of more than 1,700 bushels per acre. He ushered her to the door and refused to talk to her further about potatoes!

CHEESEY POTATOES

2 medium Kennebec potatoes
1 medium onion
2 large cloves garlic
½ teaspoon salt
⅛ teaspoon freshly ground pepper

1½ tablespoons flour
1 cup non-fat cottage cheese
2 ounces shredded Tillamook® cheddar cheese
Nonstick spray oil

Peel potatoes and cut into ½-inch chunks. Place potatoes in steamer rack over ½-inch water in deep sauce pan. Bring to boiling, then reduce heat to medium; cook about 15 minutes until potatoes can just be penetrated with fork.

Remove steamer rack with potatoes, discard water, and return potatoes to sauce pan. Add flour, spices, cottage cheese, finely diced onion and garlic, and stir well. Transfer to medium Corningware dish sprayed with nonstick oil and bake uncovered in preheated 350°F oven for 20 minutes. Add cheddar cheese and bake 10 minutes more. Makes 4 servings.

CHEESEY POTATOES

MASHED POTATOES

3–4 2½–3-inch-diameter Kennebec potatoes
¼+ cup 1% milk

Peel potatoes and cut into ¾-inch chunks. Place in steamer rack over ½-inch water in deep sauce pan. Bring to boiling, then reduce heat to medium. Cook about 15–20 minutes or until potatoes can be penetated easily with fork. Remove steamer rack with potatoes from sauce pan. Discard remaining water and return potatoes to sauce pan. Fragment potatoes with mixer set at lowest speed, add milk, and beat potatoes with mixer at medium-high speed until light and fluffy. Serve immediately.

To prepare left-over mashed potatoes, place each helping in small pryrex baking dish, break into small chunks, and cover with about ½ ounce of Tillamook® cheddar cheese. Microwave on highest setting 1 minute, turn dish 180 degrees and microwave for 1 minute more. Serve in dish.

Most mashed potatoes are made with potatoes cooked in boiling water. Not only are many of the nutrients (especially vitamin C) leached from the potatoes during the cooking process, but so is much of the flavor. So, for really tasty, nutritious mashed potatoes, always steam them.

POTATO CAKES

1½ cups left-over and chilled **MASHED POTATOES**   3–4 tablespoons canola oil
¼ cup flour   Nonstick spray oil

Pour flour onto piece of waxpaper. Spoon ¼ of potatoes onto floured paper. Coat hands with flour and form potatoes into cakes about 2½ inches in diameter and about ¾-inch thick. Make sure that cakes are well coated with flour. Spray skillet with nonstick oil, add oil and heat on medium to medium high. Saute cakes, turning once, until both sides are medium brown and crunchy. Blot on paper towel to remove excess oil before serving.

MACARONI AND CHEESE

2 cups macaroni   ¼ pound medium-sharp cheddar cheese
1½–2 quarts water   ¼ cup 1% milk
1 teaspoon salt   1 teaspoon marjoram
2 tablespoons olive oil   ½ teaspoon monosodium glutamate
¼ pound processed cheese (Velveeta®)

Bring water, salt, and olive oil to boil in 3-quart sauce pan. Add macaroni (leave uncovered) and stir occasionally until tender, about 17 minutes. Drain pasta in colander; shake to remove all of water. Melt cheese with milk in a 2-quart covered baking dish in microwave until it becomes a homogenous sauce. Grind marjoram and monosodium glutamate in mortar and pestle. Add spice and macaroni to baking dish and stir until mixed thoroughly. Microwave 1 minute to replace heat lost in mixing. Makes 5–6 servings. Leftovers can be refrigerated for a couple of days. To rewarm, place serving into pyrex dish and microwave for 1–2 minutes.

GOBBLER LASAGNA

18 pieces uncooked lasagna
1 tablespoon olive oil
1 tablespoon salt
1½ pounds ground turkey
1 cup finely chopped onion
4 large cloves garlic
2 teaspoons sugar
1 tablespoon salt
1½ teaspoons sweet basil
2 teaspoons oregano
1 teaspoon fennel seed
¼ teaspoon pepper

2 teaspoons beef bouillon
1 tablespoon Worcestershire sauce
1 quart home-canned tomatoes (drained)
1 pint home-canned tomato sauce
1½ pints non-fat, small-curd cottage cheese (drained)
1 tablespoon dried parsley flakes
1 egg white + 2 tablespoons egg substitute
   (Eggbeaters®)
½ teaspoon salt
1 pound low-fat mozzarella cheese
¾ cup shredded (not grated) Parmesan cheese
Nonstick spray oil

Drain cottage cheese in strainer overnight in refrigerator. Cook lasagna in stock pot in gallon of water, 1 tablespoon salt, and olive oil until tender (about 17 minutes). Drain pasta in colander. While pasta cooks, saute onion and garlic in 2 tablespoons olive oil over medium-high in Dutch oven; cook until onion is translucent (about 5 minutes). Add meat and brown. When moisture exudes from meat add bouillon and Worcestershire sauce; continue cooking until moisture evaporates. Grate cheese. Grind fennel in mortar and pestle. Add sugar, salt, basil, oregano, fennel, pepper, tomatoes, and tomato paste; simmer, stirring occasionally, for 20 minutes. Combine egg, cottage cheese, parsley, and ½ teaspoon salt. Spray 9- by 13-inch baking dish with nonstick oil. Spread 1 cup of meat sauce in dish, ⅓ of lasagna, ⅓ of remainder of meat sauce, ⅓ of cottage cheese mixture, ⅓ pound mozzarella cheese, ¼ cup Parmesan cheese, then repeat sequence twice more. Cover dish with foil sprayed with nonstick oil, place on cookie sheet in oven at 375°F for 25 minutes. Remove foil and continue baking for 25 minutes. Remove 10 minutes before cutting. Makes 10 servings. Freeze in microwave-safe individual-serving dishes covered with plastic wrap; reheat covered with plastic wrap at medium for 7 minutes, then uncover, split in half, reverse pieces, and heat 5 minutes on high.

KRAB LASAGNA

1 pound immitation crab meat
1 recipe **GOBBLER LASAGNA**, except delete turkey

Prepare as for **GOBBLER LASAGNA** except replace ground turkey with immitation krab meat. Do not cook krab, it is cooked already. Just saute onion and garlic, add spices, remove from heat, then mix with krab meat before layering with other ingredients.

COUSCOUS

½ cup chicken broth
¼ cup water
1 tablespoon soy sauce
1 teaspoon chicken bouillon
1 teaspoon margarine
½ cup couscous

Bring water and broth to boil, add soy sauce, margarine, bouillon, and couscous. Reduce heat to medium low, and cook 3–5 minutes until all liquid is absorbed. Stir. Serve.

This is a surprisingly tasty dish. It can be enhanced by converting to a pilaf by adding ¼ cup finely chopped mushrooms and ¼ cup finely chopped onion that have been sauted in ½ tablespoon canola oil.

FETTUCCINI

Fettuccini to fill a 1-inch-diameter hole
5–6 cups water
1 teaspoon salt
1 teaspoon olive oil
1½ tablespoons safflower margarine
2 tablespoons ground Parmesan cheese
2–3 tablespoons acidophilous yogurt

Heat salted water to boiling in large covered sauce pan. Add olive oil and fettuccini. Reduce heat slightly, but continue to boil uncovered. Cook 15–16 minutes until pasta is tender. Drain in colander. Return pasta to sauce pan, add yogurt, margarine, and Parmesan. Stir to mix. Serve immediately.

KRAB MOSTACCIOLI

1½ cups imitation krab meat
4 ounces mostaccioli
2 cloves garlic
½ medium onion
1 small green pepper
2 large mushrooms or equivalent
3–4 Roma tomatoes

1½ teaspoons basil
1½ teaspoons oregano
½ teaspoon freshly ground black pepper
2 teaspoons salt
4 tablespoons olive oil
Parmesan cheese
Nonstick spray oil

Scald tomatoes in hot water until skin begins to crack; remove skin. Chop tomatoes and other vegetables finely. Cook mostaccioli 14 minutes in boiling water to which 1 tablespoon olive oil and 1 teaspoon salt was added. Saute vegetables with spices in olive oil in wok first sprayed with non-stick oil. Heat krab in microwave about 3–4 minutes. Drain mostaccioli. Add cooked mostaccioli and krab to vegetables in wok. Stir fry 1–2 minutes. Transfer to plates and sprinkle with Parmesan cheese. Serves 2.

SPAGHETTI AND FISH UNBALLS

2 ½-pound snapper fillets
1 clove garlic
1 medium onion
6 medium mushrooms
1 tablespoon canola oil
1 pint home-canned tomato sauce
1 teaspoon basil
½ teaspoon oregano

1 teaspoon salt
1 teaspoon monosodium glutamate
⅛ teaspoon fresh-ground black pepper
Nonstick spray oil
spaghetti to fill a 1-inch-diameter hole
1½–2 quarts water
1 teaspoon salt
1 tablespoon olive oil

Spray 8- by 10-inch pyrex baking dish with nonstick oil. Remove rib bones from fish and place in baking dish skin-side down. Saute finely chopped onion and garlic, and sliced mushrooms in canola oil until onions are clear and limp. Add tomato sauce and spices and heat until hot through. Pour sauce over fish and bake uncovered at 350°F for 30 minutes. Heat salted water in small stock pot to boiling. Add olive oil and when fish is nearly half done, add spaghetti and cook uncovered 16–17 minutes. Drain spaghetti in colander. Serve fish and sauce on spaghetti. Sprinkle with Parmesan cheese.

FALAFIL CAKES

½ cup dry falafil
¾ cup water
1 teaspoon sesame oil
Nonstick spray oil

Mix dry falafil and water. Set aside for 10–15 minutes. Heat griddle over medium burners, spray with nonstick oil, and sprinkle with sesame oil. Pour falafil mixture into 4 3–4-inch diameter cakes. When browned and a bit crispy around the edges, turn and brown other side. Makes 2 servings.

This dish, although classified here as a starch, is relatively high in plant protein as it is made largely of legumes. Serve with roast chicken and steamed broccoli for a really tasty and nutritious dinner.

VEGGIES-N-DIP PLATE—page 36

SALADS

One of my first adventures in cooking after successfully preparing an edible "blade-cut" pot-roast was to add a salad to the menu. The absence of sufficient fiber in the diet of both my son and I was beginning to affect our well-being. So, off I went to the grocery store again thinking salads shouldn't be too much trouble; they only have lettuce, tomatoes, mushrooms, green onions, and a bit of cucumber. I duly purchased what seemed appropriate amounts of each. In preparing the first salads, I chopped half a head of lettuce, a couple of tomatoes, about a dozen mushrooms, half dozen green onions, and a whole cucumber. I quickly filled the bowls from which we had always eaten salads before I became the cook, so I shifted their contents to large bowls that previously had always appeared upon the dining table filled with over-cooked vegetables. On each salad, I poured on about ¼ of a bottle of dressing that remained in the refrigerator. I proudly served my son his salad and we began to consume the contents of our serving bowls while another "blade-cut" pot-roast cooked in the oven. With first salads half eaten, my son and I decided that I should be a bit more conservative with both vegetables and dressing while fixing tossed salads in the future. We each scraped the remains of our first salads into covered plastic bowls for the refrigerator. A week later, upon rediscovering the salads, we fortunately decided that the darkened and somewhat moldy contents of the plastic bowls might not be fit for human consumption.

From this humbling beginning, my tossed salads not only became somewhat smaller, but occasionally I began to add things like hulled sunflower seeds and home-made **CROUTONS** (page 10). I also began to experiment with salad dressings, first with those available in stores then with those that I concocted myself. I finally decided that a few drops of each vinegar and grape-seed oil (or olive oil) was the dressing that I preferred. Sometimes, the oil-vinegar mix was followed by a few sprinkles of grated Parmesan cheese.

And so, following experiments with tossed salads and with fiber requirements satisfied, I began to expand the menu with other salads, some containing fruit that I had canned myself. My reading of cookbooks and extension service manuals was beginning to pay off!

VEGGIES-N-DIP PLATE

1 8-ounce package of "light" cream cheese
⅔ cup cultured buttermilk
1 tablespoon soy sauce
1 tablespoon lemon juice
2 teaspoons garlic powder
1 teaspoon monosodiuim glutamate
½ teaspoon tarragon
½ teaspoon cilantro

10 large mushrooms
4 large carrots
5–6 stalks celery
20–30 small florets broccoli
20–30 small florets cauliflower
20–30 radishes
20–25 cherry tomatoes
10–15 green onions

Remove cheese from package and place in small mixing bowl; set aside for 30 minutes or more to warm to room temperature. Add liquids and blend with fork until completely smooth. Grind herbs with monosodium glutamate in mortar and pestle. Add to mixture and stir until blended. Makes 2 cups of dip.

Wash vegetables. Cut celery, zucchini, cucumbers, and carrots into ¼–⅜-inch wide strips about 3½–4 inches long. Cut mushrooms into quarters. Cut broccoli and cauliflower into ¾-inch diameter florets. Leave cherry tomotoes and radishes whole; remove most of top from onions. Of course, amounts and variety of vegetables can be adjusted.

Arrange vegetables on large plate or serving tray with dip in small bowl in center. Gather round and eat.

This is a great detactor for company while you finish cooking the main course. It can be prepared ahead of time, wrapped in plastic wrap, and stored in the refrigerator. It doesn't take as much refrigerator space as individual salads.

FRUIT-GELATIN SALAD

1 package apricot gelatin
1 11-ounce can mandrin oranges
1 6-ounce can crushed pineapple

2 bananas
½ cup boiling water
cold water

Pour powdered gelatin in 5- by 9-inch glass loaf dish. Add ½ cup boiling water and stir to dissolve gelatin. Drain oranges and pineapple into ½-cup measure; add sufficient cold water to make ½ cup and add to loaf dish. Add canned fruit and stir. Slice bananas crosswise ¼-inch thick; add to mixture and submerge bananas. Chill in refrigerator until gelatin sets. Cover with plastic wrap. I use 3–4-ounce servings for winter lunches—they are quick to prepare.

PEAR SALAD

1 package lime gelatin
1 large can pears or ¾ of a quart jar of home-canned pears
½ cup boiling water

In 5- by 9-inch glass loaf baking dish, dissolve contents of gelatin package in boiling water. Add ½ cup liquid covering pears. After mixing, add drained pears. Cover with plastic wrap and refrigerate.

CHERRY-GELATIN SALAD

1 package cherry jello
1 cup boiling water
2 cans dark (bing-type) cherries in lite syrup or 1 quart jar of home-canned cherries

Mix gelatin with boiling water. When mixed thoroughly, add 1 cup of cold juice from cherries. Add pitted cherries. Pour into fancy cut-glass bowl. Cover with plastic wrap and refrigerate until set. Serve.

This salad has become a tradition at Thanksgiving and Christmas in our household. The sweet taste of the gelatin and the slightly tart cherries compliment superbly the usual turkey-dressing-gravy main course. And, the cut-glass bowl, used only at holidays, adds a bit of elegance to the table.

COLE SLAW

½ head cabbage (size of your head) finely chopped
¼ cup cultured buttermilk
¼ cup "no-egg" mayonnaise (lite Miracle Whip®)
1 tablespoon lemon juice
½ teaspoon salt
½ teaspoon celery seed

Mix liquids and seasonings. Add to chopped cabbage. Refrigerate 1–2 hours. Serve.

LESLIE'S POTATO SALAD

4 medium white rose or new Kennebec potatoes
1 small onion
2 large stalks bok choy (celery can be substituted, but is not nearly as good)
2 eggs (use whites only, discard yolks)
1½ teaspoons French's hot-dog mustard
¼ cup "no-egg" mayonnaise (lite Miracle Whip®)
2½ tablespoons home-made **GREEN-TOMATO RELISH** (page 150)
½ teaspoon paprika
½–1 teaspoon salt
¼ teaspoon freshly ground black pepper

Scrub potatoes to remove skin or peel them and cut into ½- to ¾-inch cubes; place on steamer rack over ¾-inch water in 4-quart sauce pan. Punch tiny hole in shell of large end of eggs; place eggs on top of potatoes. Steam eggs and potatoes over boiling water until potatoes are tender (about 20 minutes). Cool potatoes and eggs. Remove shell from eggs; discard yolks. Chop egg whites, bok choy, and onion finely. Add all ingredients to potatoes and stir. Refrigerate. Makes 4 large servings.

My spouse always made this dish with celery instead of bok choy. Once, when she had the potatoes and eggs cooking and was dicing the onion, she discovered she had no celery. I suggested she substitute bok choy and ran to the garden to pull a couple of stalks. We enjoyed the change so much we revised the recipe. You can still use celery instead of bok choy as a last resort.

SALMON SALAD

½ pound left-over baked salmon or 2 4-ounce cans of red salmon
2 **HARD-BOILED EGGS** (page103; discard yolks)
1/3 cup finely chopped celery
¼ cup finely chopped onion
½ cup "no-egg" mayonnaise (lite Miracle Whip®)
1 tablespoon chopped kosher dill pickel
1 teaspoon tarragon
½ teaspoon cilantro
½ teaspoon monosodium glutamate
½ teaspoon salt
¼ teaspoon pepper

Mix ingredients throroughly. Chill and serve with sliced cucumber and a variety of crackers.

For a plate of elegant and most unusual hor-d'oeuvres, remove centers from small (1-inch diameter) lemon cucumbers with mellon baller (sharpened metal half-sphere on a handle used to make spherical servings of mellons) and fill to near overflowing with this salmon salad. This is a dish that will require that you have a garden, because not only are lemon cucumbers rare in groceries, the only ones that I've ever seen there are far too large. But, guests served these tidbits will forever consider you a master chef.

FRUIT SALAD

1 large pineapple
6 ripe bananas
4 oranges
6 kiwis
1 medium cantaloupe

1 large bunch green seedless grapes
1 large bunch red seedless grapes
3 nectarines
3–4 limes

Peel and core pineapple, peel and remove seeds from cantelope and nectarines, and peel and deseed oranges; cut all three into bite-sized chunks. Peel and slice bananas and kiwis. Remove grapes from stems and wash. Squeeze lime juice over fruit while stirring. Serves 8–10.

Whenever we are invited to a pot-luck and are designated to bring a salad, this is the recipe that we use. We may double or triple the amounts depending upon the size of the crowd expected. Admittedly, it is sort of spendy, but we have never had to bring left-over fruit salad home. For 2 servings, we use ¼ of a pineapple, 1 banana, 1 orange, and 1 kiwi, and reduce other ingredients accordingly.

Any fruit can be added or used as a substitute: pitted light or dark cherries, blueberries, raspberries, blackberries, mango, papaya, honeydew melon, peaches, etc.

CHICKEN-VEGETABLE SOUP

SOUPS

Originally, several of the soups described herein were designed to make better use of leftovers. Subsequently, I began to package and freeze small lots (½ cup each) of certain vegetables (hulled green beans, peas, lima beans, and corn) for use in vegetable soups. I also prepare and freeze broths for future use as soup stocks. See the section on **CHICKEN** (page 55) for my method of making and storing chicken broth; a similar method for preparing beef broth is described with the recipe for **BEEF-VEGETABLE SOUP** (page 42).

CHICKEN-VEGETABLE SOUP

3 cups chicken broth with meat
1 cup water
1 quart canned tomatoes
½ cup English peas
½ cup hulled green beans
½ cup lima beans
½ cup corn (dried corn may be used)
1 large potato peeled and diced
2 broccoli stems peeled and diced
¼ head of cabbage chopped

1 small green pepper diced
2 carrots scrubbed and diced
¼ cup nutritional yeast
2 tablespoons chicken bouillon
1 teaspoon tarragon
1 teaspoon cilantro
¼ teaspoon black pepper
½ cup chopped parsley (or 1 tablespoon dried parsley)
1 sprig fresh rosemary (remove before serving)
1 large onion peeled and chopped

Place all items in 4 quart or larger pot. Bring to a boil, stirring occasionally. Lower temperature and simmer for 1–1½ hours. Serve with **SOURDOUGH BAKING POWDER BISCUITS** (page 21) or **SOURDOUGH FRENCH BREAD** (page 20). Saltine crackers are a third choice. Cool leftover soup by placing pot in cold water in sink. Refrigerate and reheat servings as needed within 3 days of cooking.

CHICKEN-RICE SOUP

2 cups chicken-broth concentrate
2 cups boned roast chicken (scrap meat)
⅓ cup long-grain rice
3 cups water
1 medium onion
8–10 medium mushrooms (sliced)
1 carrot (coarsely grated)

2 cloves garlic
2 stalks celery with leaves
1 teaspoon monosodium glutamate
⅛ teaspoon black pepper (freshly ground)
1 tablespoon chicken bouillon
1 teaspoon tarragon

Chop onion, garlic, and celery. In 3-quart sauce pan, combine broth, water, chicken, rice, onion, garlic, celery, and spices. Bring to boil, stir, reduce heat, and simmer 1 hour. Makes approximately 4 servings.

BEEF-VEGETABLE SOUP

Remove stew meat and rib-eye steaks from 2 or 3 "blade-cut pot roasts" or chuck roasts, or purchase 2 "soup bones." Place bones, tendons, fat, and gristle into pressure cooker. Add 3–4 cups water. Bring pressure to 15 pounds/square inch and hold for 30 minutes. Turn off burner, but leave pan on stove until it cools completely. Pour off liquid into quart jar, refrigerate until fat hardens, then remove and discard fat. Remove meat from bones and save for soup. To ½ of liquid add:

1 quart canned tomatoes	½ tablespoon beef bouillon
1–2 cups water	1 tablespoon red wine vinegar
2 large onions, coarsely chopped	1 tablespoon Worchestershire sauce
3–4 stalks celery + some leaves coarsely chopped	1 teaspoon thyme
½ cup frozen peas	1 teaspoon basil
1 cup frozen corn	½ tablespoon salt
½ cup macaroni	

Simmer ingredients until macaroni is tender. Serve with rye rounds and cream cheese for a lucious lunch.

A large potato cut into ½-inch cubes may be substitued for macaroni. Also, canned green beans may be substituted for peas or corn. Soup, cooled quickly after cooking by placing stock pot in sink of cold water, may be refrigerated up to 3 days.

BEAN SOUP

2 cups beans
2½ quarts water
2 smoke-cured ham hocks
1 cup chopped onion
1 quart home-canned tomatoes
1 teaspoon chili powder
2 large cloves garlic
Salt to taste (you may not need any depending on how the ham hocks were cured.

I use a commercial 13-bean mix, but any multivariety combination of dried beans will do. Wash beans and soak overnight. Drain and rinse beans, add 2½ quarts water and ham hocks; cover, bring to boil, and simmer 2–2½ hours. Add onion, tomatoes, and seasonings. Simmer ½ hour longer. Makes 8 servings. Serve with cornbread.

To reduce fat, cook ham hocks in 1½ quarts of water in pressure cooker at 15 pounds/square inch for 40 minutes. Allow to cool, pour off liquid in quart jars, and refrigerate until fat congeals. Remove fat and discard. Remove meat from bones—discarding fat. Use liquid to cook beans and other vegetables.

OXTAIL-BARLEY SOUP

1½–2 pounds oxtail vertebrae with meat
1½ quarts water

Place oxtail vertebrae and water in pressure cooker. Bring pressure to 15 pounds/square inch and hold for 30 minutes. Allow pressure to fall and contents of cooker to cool slowly. When cool, remove oxtail vertebrae to plate and pour liquid into quart jars. Refrigerate liquid until fat congeals; remove fat and discard. Carefully remove meat from oxtail vertebrae; separate fat and discard. Divide broth and meat into ⅓rd's; combine ⅓ of meat and ⅓ of broth in each of 2 packages and freeze for future use.

1 pint oxtail broth	½ cup pearl barley
⅓ of oxtail meat	1 tablespoon Worchershershire sauce
1 quart water	2 teaspoons beef bouillon
1 large onion	½ teaspoon salt
2 cloves garlic	½ teaspoon thyme
1 stalk celery with leaves	½ teaspoon basil
2 cups sliced mushrooms	½ teaspoon monosodium glutamate
2 broccoli stems peeled	

Chop vegetables then place all ingredients in stock pot and simmer for 2 hours. Add water as necessary to maintain level in stock pot. Cool, refrigerate overnight, and reheat before serving. Serve with low-salt crackers and low-fat Havarti, Jack, or Mozzarella cheese. This is a hearty, stick-to-the-ribs soup for the coldest, snowest, winter day. It is well worth the trouble—and just think, 2 more batches don't require preparing the broth and meat from the oxtail vertebrae!

BROCCOLI CHOWDER

1 large potato	2 cups 1% milk
1 medium onion	2 teaspoons chicken bouillon
3–4 large florets of broccoli	¼ teaspoon ground tarragon
1 cup chicken broth	⅛ teaspoon freshly ground black pepper
1 tablespoon sesame oil	¼ cup Parmesan cheese
⅓ cup flour	½ roast breast of chicken

Peel potato and cut into ½-inch cubes and finely chop onion; place in steamer with ½ cup water, bring to a boil, reduce heat and cook for 10 minutes. Chop broccoli finely, add to steamer, and cook all vegetables 5 minutes longer. In soup pot, add chicken broth, bouillon, oil, and spices. Dice chicken (discard bones and skin) and add to soup pot; heat to simmer. Add vegetables including water from steamer. Mix flour and cold milk in separate container; add to soup pot. Add Parmesan, bring to simmer, stirring constantly. Serve when thickened. Makes 4 servings.

This recipe evolved from the **OREGON CLAM CHOWDER** (page 44) recipe. Upon discovering no clams in the pantry after having started to steam the potatoes, I made a quick trip to the refrigerator to find only a nice head of broccoli. I deleted the bacon and made some quick changes in a few other ingredients to produce a satisfying and elegant dish.

OREGON CLAM CHOWDER

2 medium potatoes (3½-inch diameter)
1 large onion
2 slices thick-sliced bacon (diced)
½ cup diced ham
½ cup flour

3 cups milk
2 teaspoons salt
½ teaspoon pepper
2 6½-ounce cans chopped clams

Peel and dice potatoes (½-inch cubes); steam pototoes until tender (cubes will break easily when pierced with a fork). Fry bacon bits in Dutch oven until crisp; pour off all but 1 teaspoon of fat. Add onion and saute until clear. Add flour, stir briefly then add milk, potatoes (including water), clams (including juice), ham, and spices. Cook over medium heat stirring constantly until thick and bubbly. Serve with saltine crackers. You won't ever buy another can of clam chowder!

OREGON CLAM CHOWDER

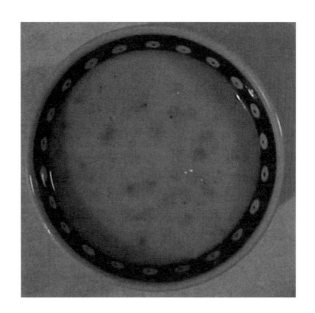

SUPER SOUP

1 cup chicken broth
½ cup cooked chicken
½ cup cooked rice
1 small onion finely chopped
2 cloves garlic finely chopped

2 teaspoons chicken bouillon
2 cups 1% milk
⅓ cup Parmesan cheese
3 tablespoons corn starch
10 stalks asparagus washed and cut into 1-inch lengths

Place asparagus in steamer and steam for 10 minutes. At same time, place first 6 items in large sauce pan and simmer for 10 minutes; pour into blender and blend until smooth (about 3–4 minutes). Return materials to sauce pan. Add corn starch to cold milk and dissolve. Add milk (with starch), cheese, and asparagus to material in sauce pan and heat over medium high while stirring constantly until thickened. Serve with low-salt crackers and low-fat Havarti, Jack, or Mozzarella cheese.

FISH CHOWDER

2 slices bacon
1 large onion
1 teaspoon salt
½ teaspoon black pepper
1 teaspoon dried basil
1 teaspoon thyme
1 bay leaf

1 tablespoon dried parsley
1½ cups boiling water
2 tablespoons lemon juice
1½ pounds snapper
1 pint canned tomatoes
2 medium potatoes

Peel and dice potatoes into ½-inch cubes; steam until just beginning to get tender (about 15 minutes). Cut bacon in ¼-inch cubes, coarsely chop onion, and fry bacon in lower half of Dutch oven until crisp. Pour off all but 1 teaspoon of fat, add bay leaf and onions; saute until onions are limp and tanslucent. Add salt and spices, stir, then add remaining ingredients including water remaining in potato steamer. Simmer, stirring occasionally, 20 minutes or until fish is completely white through. Serve with cornbread. This makes a excellent winter supper.

When invited for an evening "grading party" after a midterm exam, my teaching assistants commonly let it be known that they especially liked fish chowder, corn bread, and apple pie. They even ate the chowder after 1 of the assistants who was helping me cook misread the recipe and added 1 tablespoon of black pepper. I think that they thought that the tears the pepper brought to their eyes might delay grading the papers. I was not magnanimous—they ate my chowder, they must help grade the tests!

CARDIAC EGG-FLOWER SOUP

1 cup chicken broth
1 cup water
1 teaspoon chicken bouillon
1 teaspoon soy sauce
1 teaspoon monosodium glutamate

1 green onion
¼ cup soy bean sprouts
1 medium mushroom
1 egg white
2 tablespoons egg substitute (Eggbeaters®)

Wash and chop bean sprouts, mushroom, and onion including all but the tips of the green top of the onion. Separate white of egg into ¼-cup measure—add sufficient egg substitute (±2 tablespoons) to fill cup; stir vigorously. Heat water and broth to boiling; add bouillon, soy sauce, and vegetables, bring back to boiling; and drizzle egg mixture into boiling water-broth mixture. Serve immediately. Makes 2 servings. This is an excellent prelude to a stir-fry dinner.

ORIENTAL KRAB SOUP

2 cups concentrated chicken broth plus 1 pint water, or 2 15-ounce cans of chicken broth
1 bay leaf
¼ teaspoon black pepper
1 tablespoon chicken bouillon
juice from ½ large lime
1 large onion chopped into about 12 pieces
2 stalks celery sliced obliquely into ½-inch-wide pieces
1 medium carrot sliced ⅛-inch thick
10 small broccoli florets
10 small cauliflower florets
½ cup soy bean sprouts
12 small whole mushrooms
1½ cups imitation krab cut into ¾-inch chunks
2 tablespoons cornstarch dissolved in ¼ cup cold water

In large stockpot, bring broth, bay leaf, pepper, bouillon, and lime juice to a boil. Dump in vegetables and bring to a boil, then boil for 1–2 minutes. Add frozen krab and bring to a boil again. Add cornstarch and water and continue cooking until soup comes to a boil. Serve immediately. Goes well with sourdough scones.

CABBAGE SOUP

1 cup chicken broth
2 cups water
1 tablespoon chicken bouillon
Dash of freshly ground black pepper

1 medium onion
6 medium mushrooms
1 medium carrot
¼ medium head cabbage

Place first 4 ingredients in medium stock pot and bring to a boil. Chop onion, slice mushrooms thinly, and grate carrot coarsely. Shred cabbage with no piece larger than 1 inch on a side. Place vegetables in boiling broth, bring back to a boil, and simmer for 10 minutes. With a slice of sourdough French bread and a piece of Havarti cheese for each, this makes a nice light lunch for 2.

My spouse, while traveling in Russia in autumn, was served cabbage soup on several occasions. She enjoyed it immensely, but she could never describe precisely how the Russians made the soup. So, I put this recipe together as a trial. She said that it wasn't like the cabbage soup served in Russia, but she liked it. That's what counted!

VEGETABLES

Vegetables, in addition to fruits, are sources of vitamins, and equally important to our well-being, fiber that makes our digestive systems function properly. In our modern, "fast-food" society, the slice of onion, paper-thin slice of half-ripe tomato, and handful of chopped lettuce on our hamburger is insufficient to keep everything operating efficiently. From first-hand personal experience, I can attest that such a diet is inadequate, and if over-done, as in my case, can become life-threatening. Based on the admonishments of a series of physicians about the paucity of vegetables in my blade-cut pot-roast, carrot, and potato diet, I quickly constructed additional beds in my garden area. Broccoli, English peas, snow peas, cauliflower, zucchini, lima beans, beets, spinach, parsnips, cabbage, bok choy, and salsify were among the crops that joined carrots, potatoes, a bit of lettuce, and a couple of tomatoes in the garden and began to appear on the table in increasing volume and with increasing frequency.

My previous experience with most cooked vegetables was disgusting, if not tragic. I had to find a way to prepare those harvested from my garden beds that produced dishes sufficiently palatable that they could be ingested. I found that in steamed vegetables.

STEAMER RACK

STEAMING VEGETABLES

Steaming vegetables preserves a greater proportion of vitamins and minerals than boiling them in water. Boiling tends to leach many of the nutrients from the food and overcooking tends to destroy others. Also, boiling reduces the palatability of many vegetables.

Steaming is most easily accomplished with the folding steaming racks that fit most medium and small sauce pans and can be purchased in the kitchen-supply departments of most "mart-type"stores for a few dollars. A couple of these racks are indispensable. Interestingly, steam is the same temperature as boiling water, thus, cooking time is not reduced by raising the vegetables to be cooked out of the water.

For greatest nutrition, most vegetables should be cooked "tender-crisp"; that is, hot through and slightly limp, but still slightly crunchy when chewed. Bring ½ inch of water in sauce pan to a boil, then add vegetables in steaming rack (reduce heat to medium); approximate cooking times for steaming 2 servings of some common vegetables are as follows (allow slightly more time for greater number of servings):

Asparagus	8–10 minutes
Beets (1½ inches in diameter)	20–25 minutes
Broccoli	8–10 minutes
Cabbage (2-inch wedges)	7–8 minutes
Carrots (1-inch chunks)	15–18 minutes
Cauliflower	10–12 minutes
English peas	8–10 minutes
Green beans (whole or snapped into 1½-inch lengths)	10–12 minutes
Lima beans	20 minutes
Parsnips (½ inch chunks)	8–10 minutes
Potatoes (½-inch chunks)	15–20 minutes
Snow peas	5–6 minutes

Serve, when cooked, with a pinch of salt, or margarine added. For superb carrots, add a touch of margarine, and a pinch of each ginger and mace.

Potatoes may be scrubbed or peeled, but many of the nutrients other than carbohydrates are in or near the peel of potatoes. Scrub carrots. Beets should have the peel removed after they stick tender with a fork; run cold water over them for a few seconds to permit handling them long enough to slip the peel off with the fingers. And, leave about 2 inches of stems when cooking beets to avoid loss of color and nutrients. Cut cooked beets into chunks, add a bit of margarine, and enjoy.

ZUCCHINI CAKES

3 tablespoons flour
2 tablespoons bread crumbs
¼ cup Parmesan cheese
½ teaspoon baking powder
¼ teaspoon monosodium gultimate (optional)
1–2 teaspoons sesame oil

1 medium zucchini (grated; do not peel)
1 egg white
2 tablespoons egg substitute (Eggbeaters®)
1½ tablespoons soy sauce
Nonstick spray oil

Heat griddle over medium heat. Mix dry ingredients, added grated zucchini and liquid elements. Mix thoroughly. Spray griddle with nonstick oil; continue heating griddle until oil commences to brown. Sprinkle with sesame oil. Spoon batter onto griddle and spread into ¼-inch-thick cakes. Turn down heat to medium and cook until brown; turn cakes with pancake turner. Makes 6 cakes (serves 2).

Serve with broiled chicken, broiled or oven-fried fish, or roast turkey. Green peas, snow peas, broccoli, or spinach are excellent complimentary vegetables.

GARDEN GARBAGE

1 medium zucchini
1 medium onion
2 medium tomatoes

¼ teaspoon thyme (or a few sprigs of fresh thyme)
2 teaspoons sesame oil
Nonstick spray oil

Wash and slice zucchini crosswise in ⅛-inch-thick slices. Peel onion and slice crosswise; separate rings. Pour boiling water over tomatoes and let stand for 2–3 minutes until skin begins to slip; peel tomatoes and slice crosswise. Spray skillet with nonstick oil; add sesame oil, vegetables, and spices, and saute until zucchini slices are crisp-tender. This is a great summer vegetable dish—quick, easy, and tasty.

GARDEN GARBAGE, TOO

5 ears double-sweet sweet corn
1 medium green pepper
2 medium Early-Girl tomatoes
2 small zucchini
2 cloves garlic

2 springs fresh thyme
1½ teaspoons sesame oil
2 ounces Tillamook® cheddar cheese
Nonstick spray oil

Bring 3-inches of water in soup pot to boil. Husk corn and remove silks. Drop corn into boiling water, replace lid, and cook for 10 minutes. While corn cooks, dice peppers, tomatoes, and zucchini. Spray skillet with nonstick oil and add sesame oil; heat over medium heat. Saute peppers, tomatoes, zucchini, garlic, and thyme until zucchini is limp. Remove corn from ears and mix with other vegetables. Place into 4 individual earthenware dishes. Grate cheese on top of vegetables. Cover and microwave for 2 minutes or until cheese is melted.

STEWED TOMATOES

1 pint whole canned tomatoes
1 medium onion finely diced
1 cup finely diced celery (plus some chopped leaves)
½ cup finely diced fresh mushrooms
2 slices dark bread (rye, whole wheat, multigrain) toasted
½ teaspoon salt
⅛ teaspoon pepper
Dash of Worcestershire® sauce
1½ tablespoons canola oil
2 tablespoons flour

Slice onion, celery, and mushrooms and saute in oil until onion is clear and tender-crisp. Add flour, stir, and remove from heat; pour into 1-quart casserole. Dice toast and add about half to mixture; add tomatoes, salt, pepper, and Worcestershire® sauce, and mix gently. Add remaining diced toast. Bake in 350°F oven for 45 minutes. This is an excellent winter vegetable dish. This makes about 8 servings; it can be refrigerated and reheated quickly in the oven or microwave.

MICROWAVED ACORN SQUASH

1 4–5-inch diameter acorn squash
2 tablespoons canola oil
3–4 tablespoons dark brown sugar
¼ teaspoon freshly ground nutmeg

Cut squash in half longways and remove seeds. Place squash cut-side down in baking dish and cover with plastic wrap. Microwave on highest setting for 5 minutes; turn dish 180 degrees and microwave 5 minutes more. Remove plastic wrap and turn squash halves cut-side up. Add ½ of oil and brown sugar to cavity in each half, and sprinkle with nutmeg. Microwave uncovered on highest setting for 4 minutes more. Place large serving spoon beneath halves to move to plates. Be careful, don't burn your tongue.

SALSIFY (OYSTER PLANT) CASSEROLE

Remove cap and tip and scrape 12 large salsify roots with knife to remove hairlike roots and dirt. (Scraped roots produce milky substance that stains hands sort of purple.) Cut roots into ¾-inch segments and cook by steaming until tender (about 10 minutes). Make casserole precisely as described for **SCALLOPED OYSTERS** (page 95) except substitute salsify for oysters.

Salsify is difficult to find in grocery stores. I'm not sure that it would sell well because it looks like a large hairy white carrot. Also, to be good, salsify must have endured several frosts while it was growing. I plant a 4-foot row of salsify about mid-July in the Willamette Valley, Oregon, but usually don't harvest it until January or February. It is an interesting taste treat if you like the flavor of oysters—and it is a nice addition to the vegetable fare in midwinter.

FRIED EGGPLANT

2 Ichoban eggplants, 7–8 inches long
2–3 tablespoons egg substitute (Eggbeaters®)
bread crumbs

salt
3–4 tablespoons olive oil

Peel eggplants with potato peeler. Cut diagonally into ⅜-inch-thick slices. Sprinkle slices with salt, place on double thickness paper towel and cover with paper towel; allow to sit 15–20 minutes or until paper towels are soaked. Wash slices under running water to remove salt. Blot dry with paper towels. Dip into egg substitue, place on pile of bread crumbs, cover with bread crumbs, and press with heel of hand to make crumbs stick to eggplant. (I do the latter operation on a piece of wax paper, so that when I am finished I can pour the remaining bread crumbs back into the container.) Saute in olive oil over medium heat until crisp on each side—add oil as necessary. Blot on paper towels to remove excess oil. Serve with grated Parmesan cheese.

The salt treatment tends to reduce the amount of oil absorbed by the eggplant during frying. Small zucchinis may be prepared in the same manner, except omit the salt treatment.

BROILED EGGPLANT

2 Ichoban eggplants
1 tablespoon salt
2 teaspoons olive oil
½ teaspoon oregano

½ teaspoon monosodium glutamate
2–3 tablespoons grated Parmesan cheese
Nonstick spray oil

Peel eggplants with potato peeler then split in half lengthwise. Sprinkle heavily with salt; place on double-thickness paper towels, cover with double-thickness paper towels, and allow to sit for 30 minutes. Wash eggplants under running cold water to remove salt; pat dry with paper towels. Coat each piece of eggplant with ½ teaspoon olive oil poured into palm of hand. Place flat side down on broiler pan sprayed with nonstick oil and broil about 4–5 minutes or until eggplant begins to change color. Grind oregano and monosodium glutamate with mortar and pestle. Turn flat side of eggplant up, sprinkle lightly with finely ground oregano mixture and heavily with Parmesan cheese. Broil about 2–3 minutes or until cheese begins to brown. Serves 2.

One of my former students who was served this dish for dinner 1 summer evening referred to broiled egg plants as "slugs." We have always called this dish by her suggested name, but I hesitate to use it as a title for the recipe. It was the shape of the sliced Ichoban eggplants, not the taste that suggested the unappealing name.

BRAISED PARSNIPS

6 parsnips about 1 inch in diameter at the top   2–3 tablespoons dark brown sugar
1 tablespoon margarine   ¼ teaspoon paprika

Scrub parsnips with vegetable brush and cut into 3-inch lengths; split the larger diameter pieces lengthwise. Place in steamer and steam for 10 minutes. Place pieces in shallow baking dish containing melted margarine. Turn each piece to coat with margarine. Sprinkle with brown sugar and paprika and bake uncovered in 350°F oven for 15 minutes. Parsnips are best if harvested after several hard frosts. Those found in grocery stores in autumn are not very good.

SAUTED PARSNIPS

8 parsnips about 1 inch in diameter at the top
2 tablespoons sesame oil
Nonstick spray oil
Salt

Scrub parsnips with vegetable brush and cut into 3-inch lengths; split the larger diameter pieces lengthwise. Place in steamer and steam for 10 minutes. Spray skillet with nonstick oil add sesame oil and heat on medium burner. Transfer parsnips and saute, turning with spatula until parts of each piece are lightly browned. Serve immediately. Salt to taste.

SAUTED PARSNIPS

STUFFED MUSHROOMS

8 large white mushrooms
20–25 very small green beans
1½ ounces Tillamook® cheddar cheese
1 tablespoon olive oil
Nonstick spray oil

Remove stems from green beans and cut into ¼–⅜-inch lengths; place in steamer and steam for 10 minutes. If possible, select mushrooms with caps that have not separated from stems. With sharp knife, cut around caps of mushrooms at an angle to remove stems and leave an indentation in base of caps. Wipe outside of mushrooms with olive oil and place on small broiler pan sprayed with nonstick oil. Fill mushrooms with green beans and place ⅛-inch-thick slice of cheese on top. Place 3–4 inches below broiler element for about 5 minutes or until cheese is melted through beans and has begun to brown. Serve immediately.

CANDIED YAMS

5–6 yams or sweet potatoes
½ cup dark brown sugar

2+ tablespoons canola oil
Nonstick spray oil

Wash yams and poke them with a fork to allow steam to escape. Steam yams on rack in medium stock pot until tender when stuck with fork (about 30 minutes). Chill yams then remove skins and slice crosswise into ¼-inch thick slices. Spray heavy cast-iron skillet with nonstick oil, add canola oil, and 1/3 cup brown sugar. Heat over medium burner until sugar begins to dissolve. Place 1 layer of sliced yams on top of sugar. Saute until slices commence to brown, turn slices to other side with spatula, and continue cooking until lightly brown. Remove to warm bowl. Repeat with remaining slices adding sugar to skillet as needed. Reduce temperature as needed to avoid burning sugar. Yield is sufficient for 5–6 people; may be refrigerated and rewarmed in microwave.

ROASTED STAND-UP CHICKEN—page 58

CHICKEN

As a child of the Great Depression, I was taught frugality and I have practiced conservation both professionally and privately throughout my adult life. For example, I purchase half dozen or so frying chickens when they are on sale, prepare them for cooking, and freeze them for future use. I prepare them by removing the tail and excess skin and fat at front and rear openings, then either split them in half or leave them whole for roasting, or disjoint them for broiling (see photos on pages 56–57, 59, & 61, respectively). I always remove the kidneys and check for lungs that sometimes aren't removed by the butcher. Because I like the flavor it imparts, I add ⅛- to ¼-cup of soy sauce to each package before freezing the chicken. I double-bag and place a frozen chicken in a kitchen sink full of cold water to thaw when I need to cook 1 of them.

Necks, wingtips, gizzards, and hearts get packaged and frozen separately; livers are discared because of their high cholesterol content. When sufficient volume of these materials is obtained (parts from 6 birds is sufficient) it is placed in a pressure cooker with ample water, a tablespoon or so of vinegar, and pressured at 15 pounds for 30–40 minutes. The vinegar makes the water slightly acid so it will dissolve more nutrients from the bones; it does not impart a taste to the broth. When cooled to room temperature, then refrigerated overnight, the solidified fat can be scraped off. The broth is then melted and poured off. The meat is removed from the neck bones and the gristle removed from gizzards; this meat, in addition to the hearts, is chopped, packaged with the broth in 2-cup containers, and frozen for future use as soup stock. Care is taken in removing meat from the dorsal part of neck as tiny bones often are attached to the meat. Wing tips, remaining bones, and gristles are run through the food grinder; a couple of tablespoons of the ground material in each pan of dog food puts smiles on the faces of my springer spaniels.

I also purchase chicken legs when they are on sale, remove the skin and fat (see photos on page 65), and freeze them with soy sauce, 8 legs to a quart freezer bag. These can be broiled or used in several recipes included herein.

After preparing chickens I always clean the cutting board, knife, sink, and counter top with laundry bleach to avoid the possibility of contamination with bacteria that can cause severe gastrointestinal distress or worse. I always wear old jeans when preparing chickens as evidenced by the white splotches down the front where bleach has spattered during cleaning.

Cleaning and Preparation of A Whole Chicken

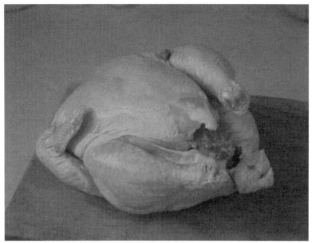

Step 1.—Unwrap chicken on cutting board; remove neck and other parts packed inside.

Step 2.—Cut off wing tips.

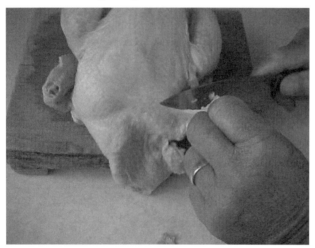

Step 3.—Remove fat and excess skin from breast regions.

Step 4.—Remove fat and excess skin from neck region.

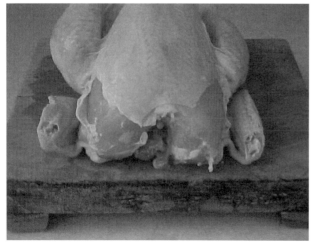

Step 5.— Front of chicken with fat and excess skin removed.

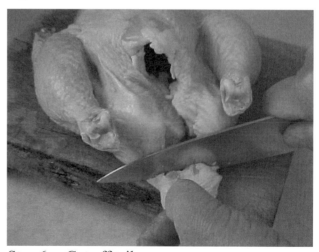

Step 6.—Cut off tail.

CLEANING AND PREPARATION OF A WHOLE CHICKEN

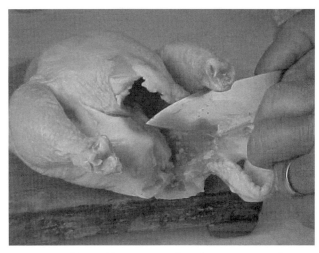

Step 7.—Cut off excess fat from around rear opening.

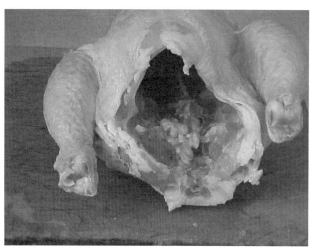

Step 8.—Rear opening of bird ready to have kidneys and reproductive organs removed.

Step 9.—Stand-up rack in broiler pan ready for chicken.

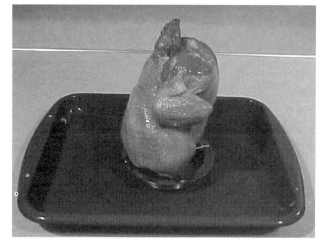

Step 10.—Chicken set on stand-up rack ready to be placed in oven for cooking.

ROAST CHICKEN

4½-pound fryer chicken
½ teaspoon tarragon
½ teaspoon cilantro
¼ teaspoon monosodium glutamate (optional)
½ teaspoon rosemary (or 1 3-inch sprig of fresh rosemary)
Nonstick spray oil

Thaw and drain whole chicken (see description and photos on pages 56–57 for preparation techniques) marinated in soy sauce while frozen. Grind tarragon, cilantro, and monosodium glutamate together with mortar and pestle; sprinkle evenly on chicken. Place rosemary in cavity. Spray sides of roasting pan with spray oil. Place chicken in roasting pan, cover, and bake at 325°F for 1 hour. Remove cover, pour off liquid, and bake uncovered for 30 minutes more.

Chicken should be tender and juicy, not dry. This is a meat dish that will provide 4 large servings for dinner plus sufficient "scappy" pieces for a chicken sandwich or 2 for lunches. The herbs give the meat a superb flavor.

STANDUP CHICKEN

4½-pound frying chicken
1 tablespoon sesame oil

Thaw and drain whole chicken (see description and photos on pages 56–57 for preparation techniques) that has been marinated in soy sauce while frozen. Preheat oven to 400°F. Place bird on upright rack set in bottom half of broiler pan (photo on page 57). Place pan on bottom rack in oven and set timer for 20 minutes. Remove bird from oven and brush with sesame oil; make sure that entire bird is covered. Return bird to oven and bake for 1 hour at 400°F.

Two people are required to remove chicken from upright rack safely. One must hold down the bottom of the rack; the other uses fork and tongs to lift bird from rack.

This is the most luscious roast chicken you ever saw or tasted; it is a beautiful golden brown with crispy skin and tender moist meat. You will be the envy of every cook in town that sees or tastes your **STANDUP CHICKEN**. However, nothing this good could come without a price. Make this dish just before you plan to clean your oven because, in roasting, the chicken does a bit of spattering.

And, again, you have 30–40 minutes to accomplish necessary chores or just relax before having to steam vegetables to accompany the chicken.

SPLIT CHICKEN

1 3–4 pound chicken
1–2 tablespoons sesame oil
Nonstick spray oil

Prepare chicken by removing excess fat and skin (photos on pages 56–57), splitting in half (photos below), and marinating in soy sauce (may be frozen with soy sauce). Place cooling rack in bottom half of broiler pan and arrange split chicken skin-side down. Place in oven preheated to 400°F for 20 minutes. Brush chicken halves with sesame oil and turn skin side up on rack. Bake at 400°F for 50 minutes longer. This is a easy dish to prepare and you have about 40 minutes to watch Monday-night football, feed the dogs, or work in the garden before having to steam the vegetables.

Left-over chicken can be reheated in the microwave or wrapped in foil and placed in a 350°F oven for 10 minutes. It is edible, but the process seems to make it a bit dry. I often bone and chop uneaten chicken and freeze it for inclusion in a **CHICKEN CASSEROLE** (page 63), **YUNG CHOW FRIED RICE** (page 100), or 1 of the chicken soups (pages 41 & 44).

PREPARATION OF A SPLIT CHICKEN

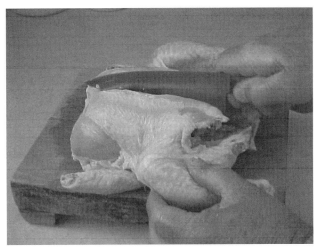

Step 1.—After removing excess fat and skin, split breast.

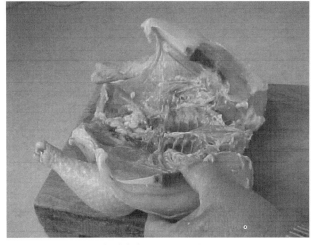

Step 2.—Spread chicken open.

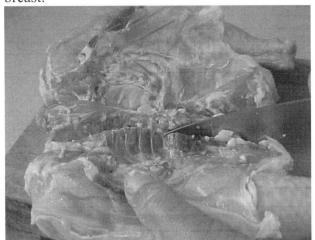

Step 3.—Split chicken by cutting alongside backbone; remove remaining neck.

BROILED CHICKEN

1 3–4 pound chicken fryer
¼ cup sesame oil
¼ cup lemon juice
½ cup soy sauce
3–4 cloves garlic
3–4 ⅛-inch slices ginger root

1 teaspoon monosodium glutamate (optional)
⅛ teaspoon pepper
1 teaspoon cilantro
1 teaspoon tarragon
Nonstick spray oil

Heat oil on medium burner; add peeled and diced garlic and diced ginger root and saute briefly (too much heat destroys garlic flavor). Quickly add lemon juice and soy sauce to cool oil. Add pepper and let cool.

Disjoint and cut chicken into serving pieces; remove excess fat and skin containing large amounts of fat (see description and photos on pages 56–57 & 61 for preparation techniques). Arrange chicken in 9- by 13-inch baking dish. Spoon about ⅓ of marinade onto chicken, stirring marinade between each spoonful. Turn chicken several times to insure that it is coated thoroughly. Marinade may be applied 30-minutes before broiling or baking dish can be covered with plastic wrap and placed in the refrigerator overnight before broiling chicken; if the latter, turn chicken in marinade at least once.

Turn chicken to ensure that it is covered with marinade. Sprinkle both sides of chicken with cilantro and tarragon that have been ground with mortar and pestle. I use monosodium glutamate for an abrasive when grinding spices. Spray broiler pan with nonstick oil. Arrange chicken cut-side up. Place about 6 inches from broiler for 17–20 minutes or until it is lightly browned; brush chicken with marinade remaining in baking dish and return to broiler with skin-side up for about 5–7 minutes or until lightly browned. Different broilers require different distances and broiling times; it is best to broil a little on the slow side (greater distances and less time) to avoid burning chicken until timing for broiling can be determined by trial and error. However, broiling too slowly produces excessively dry chicken.

Serve with **STEAMED RICE** (page 25) and broccoli in cool weather, with **LESLIE'S POTATO SALAD** (page 38) and **COLE SLAW** (page 37) in hot weather. Also, cold broiled chicken is great as a snack or in lunches. Unused marinade can be stored in the refrigerator for 2–3 weeks; it is also good brushed on salmon before broiling or grilling over charcoal.

PREPARING AND CLEANING A CUT-UP CHICKEN

Step 1.— After removing fat and excess skin (pages 56–57), remove legs at hip joint.

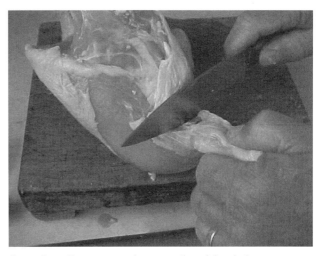

Step 2.—Remove wings at shoulder joint.

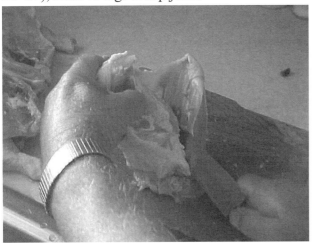

Step 3.—Remove breast from back by cutting through ribs, then

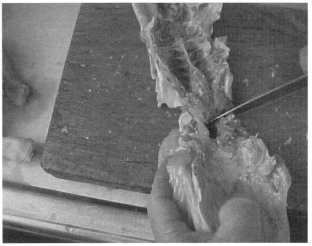

Step 4.—Cut through shoulder joint to free breast.

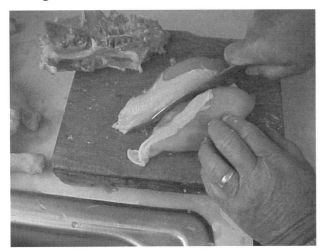

Step 5.—Split breast in half.

Step 6.—Cut back into 2 pieces.

PREPARING AND CLEANING A CUT-UP CHICKEN

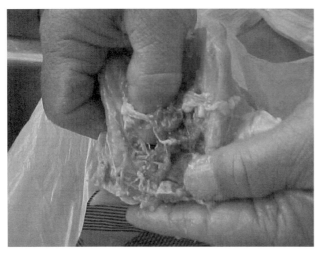

Step 7.—Remove kidneys with thumbnail.

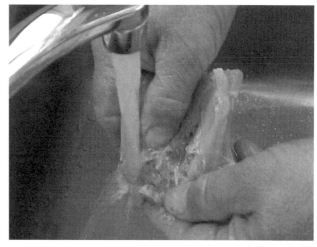

Step 8.—Wash to remove fragments of kidneys.

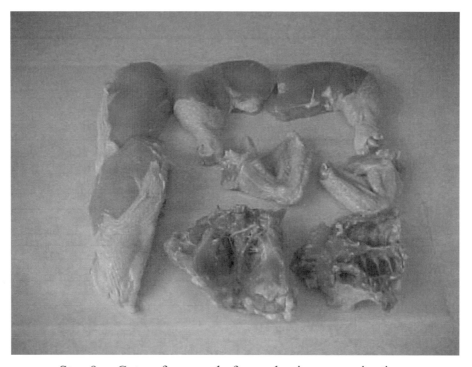

Step 9.—Cut up fryer ready for packaging or marinating.

LEFT-OVER ROAST CHICKEN AND GRAVY

½ breast and 1 thigh left-over roast chicken
1½ cups cold water
1½ tablespoons cornstarch
1 small onion
3 medium mushrooms
½ green pepper

½ teaspoon tarragon
½ teaspoon cilantro
½ teaspoon monosodium glutamate
½ tablespoon canola oil
Nonstick spray oil

Remove meat from bones and cut into ½-inch cubes. Grind spices in mortar and pestle with monosodium glutimate. Chop vegetables finely and saute in canola oil in medium sauce pan sprayed with nonstick oil. Dissolve cornstarch in cold water and add to vegetables in sauce pan. Heat over medium-high heat stirring constantly until gravy becomes thick and bubbly. Add spices and chicken and continue to stir until chicken is hot through. Serve with **STEAMED RICE** (page 25) and a steamed green vegetable.

When in a hurry, I microwave left-over roast chicken, but the process leaves the chicken a bit dry and a little tough even when covered to trap the moisture. This recipe is a way to reheat the chicken and maintain the texture of the original roast chicken. It's tasty, too.

CHICKEN CASSEROLE

2 cups left-over diced roast chicken with bones and skin removed
1 cup sliced mushrooms
½ cup finely chopped onion
2 cups (dry-measure) eggless noodles (cooked)
2 cups **CHEESEY CREAM SAUCE** (page 109)
1 teaspoon salt
1 tablespoon olive oil
Nonstick spray oil

Boil noodles for 17 minutes in 2 quarts water to which salt and olive oil were added.

In 1¾-quart Corningware dish sprayed with nonstick oil, layer materials as follows: ½ of chicken, ½ of mushrooms, ½ of onion, and noodles, then remaining chicken, mushrooms, and onion. Add cheese sauce with spices and run blade of dinner knife along edges and several places in center of casserole to allow penetration of sauce. Bake 45 minutes at 350°F.

An option, if you can stand the added cholesterol, is to sprinkle 1 cup grated Tillamook© cheddar cheese to the top 15 minutes before removing casserole from oven.

YORKSHIRE CHICKEN

8 chicken legs
3–4 tablespoons canola oil
1¼ cups flour
½ tablespoon salt
¼ teaspoon pepper, freshly ground
1 teaspoon sage

1 teaspoon baking powder
3 egg whites
⅓ cup egg substitute (Eggbeaters®)
1¼ cups milk
Nonstick spray oil

Place ¼ cup flour, ½ teaspoon salt, and the pepper in the plastic bag; shake 2–3 chicken legs (see description and photos on page 64 for preparation techniques) in bag with mixture at a time. Brown chicken on all sides in oil in large frying pan over medium-high heat. Blot browned legs with paper towels to remove excess oil. Place chicken in 9- by 13-inch baking dish sprayed with nonstick oil. Put remaining ingredients (including the remaining salt) into blender (add flour and baking powder last) and blend on high speed until lightly frothy. Pour over chcken and bake uncovered for 1 hour at 350°F. Serve with steamed broccoli or English peas. This is a great winter dish.

ROAST CORNISH HENS WITH CURRIED-RICE STUFFING

4 20–22 ounce Cornish hens
2–3 tablespoons soy sauce
1–2 tablespoons sesame oil
½ cup finely chopped onion
1 cup finely chopped mushrooms
1 tablespoon curry powder
½ cup white wine
⅓ cup raisins
¼ cup chopped parsley (or 1 tablespoon dried parsley flakes)
1 tablespoon dark brown sugar
dash garlic powder
½ cup rice cooked in 1¼ cups water + ½ teaspoon salt over medium heat for
    22 minutes or until barely dry
1–2 tablespoons canola oil

Remove tail, kidneys, and skin and excess fat from rear and neck regions (see description and photos on pages 56–57 for preparation techniques). Place hens in plastic bag with soy sauce and refrigerate for 4–5 hours or over-night. Turn hens several times to redistribute soy sauce.

Saute onion and mushrooms in canola oil over medium heat until onion is limp and translucent. Add remaining ingredients and stir until well mixed. Stuff body cavities of hens. Bake hens at 400°F for 10 minutes, then coat with sesame oil and bake for an additional 50 minutes.

PREPARATION OF DRUMSTICKS

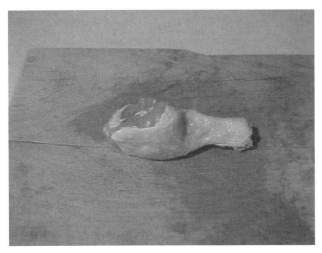

Step 1.—Place chicken leg on cutting board cut-side up.

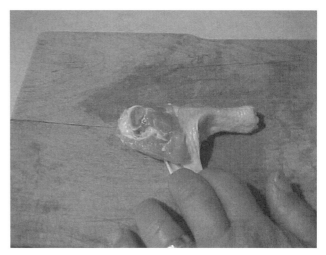

Step 2.—Pull skin away from muscles.

Step 3.—Cut skin, then press blade of knife sideways against leg and saw back and forth to remove skin and fat.

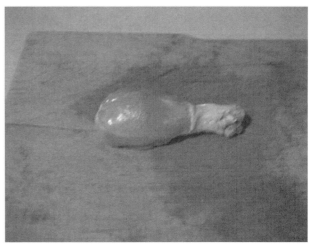

Step 4.—Leg with skin and fat removed.

RED AND GREEN CHICKEN

1 3–4 pound fryer	2 medium onions or 4 green onions
3 tablespoons flour	2 medium green peppers
1 tablespoon cornstarch	4 large tomatoes
2 teaspoons salt	½ teaspoon oregano
⅛ teaspoon pepper	2–3 tablespoons canola oil (or grape-seed oil)
2 medium zucchinis	Nonstick spray oil

Prepare chicken as for broiling (see description and photos on pages 56–57 & 61–62). Mix flour, cornstarch, and half of the salt in plastic bag. Shake 1 or 2 pieces of chicken in plastic bag to coat with flour mixture. Spray large skillet with nonstick oil, add canola oil and heat over medium-high burner; brown chicken on all sides. Blot browned chicken with paper towels to remove excess oil. Arrange chicken in 9- by 13-inch baking dish.

Cover tomatoes with boiling water for 2–4 minutes until skin slips; peel and cut tomatoes into ¾-inch chunks. Wash remaining vegetables and cut into similar-sized chunks. Distribute vegetables, pepper, and remaining salt over chicken. Cover with foil and bake in 350°F oven for 30 minutes.

Serve with **MASHED POTATOES** (page 30), **STEAMED RICE** (page 25), **FETTUCCINI** (page 32), **COUSCOUS** (page 32), or other starch.

SHAKE-COATED CHICKEN

⅓ cup Parmesan cheese	⅛ teaspoon pepper
⅓ cup bread crumbs	1 tablespoon egg substitute (Eggbeaters®)
½ teaspoon tarragon	1 tablespoon milk
½ teaspoon cilantro	3 skinned bone-in chicken breasts
½ teaspoon garlic powder	Nonstick spray oil
¼ teaspoon salt	

Grind tarragon and cilantro in mortar and pestle. Put all dry ingredients into plastic bag. Mix egg substitute and milk in mixing bowl sufficiently large to accomodate chicken breasts 1 at a time. Coat chicken breasts with liquid completely, shake to remove excess, and shake in bag and press against dry ingredients to coat thoroughly. Place on broiling pan coated sprayed with nonstick oil. Bake in 400°F oven for 35 minutes.

This chicken dish goes well with **FETTUCCINI** (page 32), **STEAMED RICE** (page 25), or a potato dish. Steamed broccoli, English peas, green beans, or other green vegetable completes an easy-to-fix and elegant meal.

BARBECUED CHICKEN

1 cut-up fryer chicken or 8 fryer drumsticks (skinned)
3 tablespoons dark brown sugar
1 tablespoon cornstarch
¾ cup pineapple juice
3 tablespoons catsup
¼ cup vinegar

1 teaspoon ground ginger
⅛ teaspoon allspice
1 tablespoon chili powder
1 tablespoon soy sauce
2 cloves garlic
Nonstick spray oil

In 1½-quart saucepan, mix pineapple juice, catsup, vinegar, spices, sugar, and cornstarch. Cook over medium heat stirring constantly until thickened. Dry chicken with paper towels. Line 9- by 13-inch baking dish with foil; spray with nonstick oil. Place chicken skin-side down in prepared baking dish. Brush chicken with half of the sauce. Bake at 400°F for 25 minutes. Turn chicken, brush with remaining sauce and bake for 40 minutes.

SWEET-AND-SOUR DRUMS

8 chicken drumsticks (skinned)
¼ cup sugar
⅓ cup apple-cider vinegar
3 tablespoons soy sauce

3 tablespoons catsup
±¼ cup cornstarch
3–4 tablespoons canola oil
Nonstick spray oil

Thaw chicken drumsticks (see photos on page 65 for preparation techniques) marinated with soy sauce while frozen. Place cornstarch in 1 gallon plastic bag. Add drumsticks 2 at a time and shake until completely covered. Heat oil in skillet first sprayed with nonstick oil on medium-high burner and brown drumsticks for 2–3 minutes on each of the 4 sides. Remove drumsticks from skillet, blot with paper towel to remove oil, and place in 8- by 8-inch pyrex baking dish. Mix sugar, vinegar, soy sauce, and catsup, and pour over chicken. Place uncovered in oven preheated to 350°F for 15 minutes, turn drumsticks, and bake for 15 additional minutes. Serve with **STEAMED RICE** (page 25) and steamed vegetable.

SWEET-AND-SOUR DRUMS

OREGANO CHICKEN

1 cup bread crumbs
¾ cup grated Parmesan cheese
1½ tablespoons oregano, freshly ground
1 teaspoon salt

⅛ teaspoon freshly ground black pepper
2–3 tablespoons egg substitute (Eggbeaters®)
10 chicken legs and thighs, attached
Nonstick spray oil

Remove heavy fat deposits and thickened skin from legs and thighs. Place bread crumbs, cheese, oregano, salt, and pepper into gallon-size plastic bag. Roll chicken pieces in half-dollar size drops of egg substitute in shallow mixing bowl until coated then place in bag and press crumb mixture into chicken. Spray broiler pan with nonstick oil. Place chicken on broiler rack and bake for 40 minutes at 350°F. Chicken should be tender with a crisp coating.

BUTTERMILK CHICKEN

8 chicken legs (skinned)
¼ cup bread crumbs
½ teaspoon thyme
1 teaspoon oregano

¼ cup dry buttermilk
1–2 tablespoons egg substitute (Eggbeaters®)
Nonstick spray oil

Combine dry ingredients in 1 gallon plastic bag; shake to mix. Remove excess skin and fat from chicken legs or thaw legs marinated with soy sauce while frozen (see photos on page 65 for preparation techniques). Coat legs with egg substitute and place, 2 at a time, in bag with dry ingredients. Shake bag and press on bag to coat legs heavily. Spray broiler pan with nonstick oil. Place legs on broiler and bake at 400°F for 35 minutes.

JICAMA CHICKEN

1 boneless and skinless chicken breast
1 tablespoon cornstarch
4 tablespoons olive oil
1 large onion
8 medium mushrooms
1 3½-inch jicama root

2 tablespoons white wine
½ cup 1% milk
½ teaspoon salt
⅛ teaspoon freshly ground black pepper
Nonstick spray oil

Slice onion, mushrooms, and peeled jicama ⅛-inch thick; cut jicama slices into ¼-inch-wide strips. Slice chicken breast into ½-inch-wide strips. Place chicken strips, cornstarch, salt, and pepper into plastic bag; shake bag to coat chicken. Spray wok with nonstick oil, add about ½ of olive oil and heat over medium-high burner. Stir-fry chicken, tossing frequently, until lightly brown and firm. Place cooked chicken in oven to keep warm. Stir-fry vegetables in remaining oil until hot through but still crisp. Add wine and stir until evaporated. Return chicken to wok, add milk and stir until sauce forms. Serve with **STEAMED RICE** (page 25) or **FETTUCCINI** (page 32).

TURKEY

By Thanksgiving, after becoming a single again, I was sufficiently adept at cooking that our survival was no longer in question. I could cook a blade-cut pot-roast with vegetables, broil chicken, bake oatmeal cookies, steam broccoli, and make bread from a recipe found on a bag of flour. The holiday was a time to expand my culinary horizons. So, I bought a 14-pound turkey with a plastic device inserted in the breast that indicated when the bird had roasted sufficiently. Instructions on the plastic wrap were reasonably straightforward: bake uncovered in an oven preheated to 425°F for 25–30 minutes, cover bird with aluminum foil, reduce heat to 325°F, and continue to bake for 20 minutes per pound or until plastic device indicated the bird was done. Let's see, 14 times 20 is 280, divided by 60 is a little over 4½ hours. The package also included a warning to remove giblets from both the body cavity and from beneath the flap of skin at the neck.

The latter admonishment likely was unread by a Midwestern relative who invited my new bride and me for Thanksgiving dinner several years after my initial attempt at roasting a turkey. Each subsequent Thanksgiving, my spouse laughs when she recalls how, after an enormous dinner with all the family gathered, she found, while helping with left-overs, the well-cooked liver, heart, and gizzard still wrapped in plastic beneath the flap of skin at the neck of the turkey. She was able to dispose of the package of cooked giblets without anyone noticing. Actually, no harm was done, but attention to the oversight would have been embarassing to my relative.

No wonder turkey is the meat of the day on Thanksgiving; roasting time permits watching a complete college football game without interruption—or so I thought. At 3½ hours, I checked the plastic device inserted in the turkey's breast; it already indicated that the bird was done. Now what? My bird was done, the dressing hadn't been baked (instructions on the package advised against stuffing the bird), the potatoes weren't peeled, and the broccoli was still in the refrigerator. Pretty simple. I recovered the bird with the foil and placed it over the back burner where heat exhausted from the oven kept it warm. I put the dressing in the oven and set the timer for 45 minutes, peeled the potatoes and put them on to steam, and prepared the broccoli for steaming 10 minutes before the potatoes were mashed. I had prepared dessert and my favorite **CHERRY-GELATIN FRUIT SALAD** (page 37) the night before. My guest arrived as I was setting the table and the meal was ready a few minutes later. The only problem was that I missed the last quarter of the Notre Dame-Michigan football game. But, my son, my guest, and I ate with a holiday spirit.

WARNING! A 14-pound turkey for 3 people is the epitome of overkill! After that sumptuous first Thanksgiving dinner an enormous pile of boned turkey was packaged for the refrigerator. During the following week, my son and I ate left-over turkey sliced with dressing and gravy, left-over turkey sandwiches, left-over turkey diced in cream sauce, left-over turkey hash, left-over turkey replacing chicken in a casserole, and I finally put the remaining left-over turkey in a plastic bag for the freezer. A couple of weeks later, when I hadn't been to the grocery for several days, I got some of the left-over turkey out of the freezer and thawed it in anticipation of serving it for dinner. My son came home from school, saw the turkey, and immediately left for his mother's house. I took a second look at the remaining turkey, served it to my springer spaniels, and dined at a nearby Chinese restaurant. And, the next morning, my son and I agreed to have blade-cut pot-roast for Christmas dinner.

Even a 6- or 7-pound turkey hen likely will produce too many left-overs when only 2 or 3 people are served at the primary meal. However, turkey is packaged in a variety of ways other than whole birds: half turkeys, turkey breasts or half breasts, turkey hindquarters, turkey tenders (sometimes referred to as turkey fillets which actually are the supra-coracoideus muscles; the ones that raise the wings in wild turkeys and other flying birds), turkey shoulders, and ground turkey are available in many groceries. Most of my recipes take advantage of these smaller amounts of turkey, but I must include a couple of ways to fix whole turkeys in the event that you decide to feed the entire clan.

APPLE-ROASTED TURKEY

1 8–10-pound young turkey   ½ cup soy sauce
4 cups unsweetened and unfiltered cider   4–6 tablespoons corn starch

Remove packages of giblets, kidneys, excess fat, loose skin, and other extraneous material from turkey. Place turkey on rack and set rack in broiler pan. Brown in preheated 425°F oven for 25 minutes. Combine 3½ cups of cider with soy sauce and pour over turkey. Cover turkey tightly with aluminum foil and roast at 325°F for about 20 minutes per pound. Baste occasionally with liquid in pan (at least once each hour).

Remove rack and turkey from broiler pan, then pour liquid into jar. Use turkey baster to transfer all but fat to sauce pan. Mix corn starch with the remaining ½ cup of cold cider. Add to liquid in sauce pan; cook until thickened, stirring constantly. Serve as gravy.

ROAST TURKEY OPTIONS

For larger turkeys, increase ingredients proportionally. For a 3–4-pound turkey breast, reduce volume of cider to 3½ cups (saving ½ cup to dissolve corn starch for gravy) and reduce soy sauce and corn starch by one-half. Roast breast with oven times calculated as for whole turkey.

One year, we decided not to have turkey, but to substitute a 5½-pound chicken. I used the same recipe, but reduced the cider by 1 cup, the soy sauce by ¼ cup, and cooking time to 1¾ hours. It was a great substitute.

**APPLE-ROASTED
TURKEY BREAST**

CORNED TURKEY

2 turkey hindquarters
½ cup salt
2 tablespoons dark brown sugar

1 tablespoon pickling spice
2 large cloves garlic
1 quart water

Dissolve salt and sugar in hot water; add spices and let cool. Remove skin from turkey parts; separate legs from thighs. Place turkey parts in gallon-size zip-lock plastic bag; add brine, close bag, and massage thoroughly. Place bag inside another plastic bag and close; refrigerate 2–4 days, turning and massaging meat twice daily. Discard brine, wash turkey with cold running water, massaging to remove excess brine. Put turkey in stock pot and add water to cover. Bring to boil, then reduce heat; simmer until meat can be removed from bones easily, about 1–1½ hours. Add carrots, potatoes, and onions for last 45 minutes. Serve in same manner as corned beef. Left-over turkey can be eaten cold as in Reuben sandwiches.

STIR-FRY TURKEY

1 pound boned turkey breast or 2 turkey tenders
1 tablespoon soy sauce
2 tablespoons sesame oil

1 recipe **TURKEY TEMPURA**
Nonstick spray oil

TURKEY TEMPURA

½ cup flour
2 tablespoons rice flour
2 tablespoons dried buttermilk
1 teaspoon garlic powder
1 teaspoon poultry seasoning

1 teaspoon monosodium glutamate
2 teaspoons salt
½ teaspoon freshly ground black pepper
1 teaspoon baking powder
1 tablespoon garlic powder

Place dry ingredients in gallon-size plastic bag; shake bag to mix. Cut turkey into 1-inch cubes. Sprinkle turkey with soy sauce and mix thoroughly to coat all sides; let set for 10 minutes. Place about ½ of cubes into bag, inflate bag, and shake bag to coat turkey with tempura. Heat oil in wok over high heat. Stir-fry turkey cubes until golden brown. Drain on paper towels. Serve with **STEAMED RICE** (page 25) and a steamed green vegetable.

SAUTED TURKEY STEAK

1 turkey tender (sometimes called turkey fillet)   2–3 tablespoons sesame oil
¼ cup **TURKEY TEMPURA** (page 71)   Nonstick spray oil
1–2 teaspoons egg substitute (Eggbeaters®)

Commencing at the large (anterior) end of turkey tender, slice into ⅜-inch-thick slices perpendicular to the muscle fibers. Remove tendon (white part). Extra slices may be wrapped in wax paper, 2 slices to a package and placed in plastic bags and frozen.

Spread layer of tempura on wax paper. Coat turkey steaks with egg substitute then dredge turkey steaks through tempura until they are well coated. Spray large skillet with nonstick oil, add sesame oil, and heat over medium burner; saute steaks until they are just done through (overcooking makes steaks dry and tough). Blot with paper towel to remove excess oil. Save unused tempura for next time.

As an alternative, pour **CHEESEY CREAM SAUCE** (page 109) over cooked steak before serving.

TURKEY GIBLET GRAVY

Meat from turkey neck, heart, and gizzard, chopped (meat from chicken parts may be added if desired)
2 **HARD-BOILED EGGS** (page 103; discard yolks)
¼ cup chopped onions
½ cup chopped mushrooms
½–1 cup drippings from roast turkey (fat removed)
2 cups broth from cooking giblets in pressure cooker (fat removed)
1 teaspoon salt
⅛ teaspoon black pepper, freshly ground
2 tablespoons corn starch
¼ cup cold water
1 tablespoon canola oil

Place neck (skinned), gizzard, and heart in pressure cooker with 1½ quarts of water and cook at 15 pounds per square inch for 30 minutes. Pour remaining liquid into quart jar and cool in cold water, then refrigerate over night. Skim off fat on surface. Pick meat from neck. Chop heart, gizzard and neck meat finely.

Saute onion and mushrooms in oil in 2-quart sauce pan until onion is limp and translucent. Add defatted liquid, chopped meat, egg, and spices. Heat on medium-high burner until liquid commences to bubble. Mix corn starch and **COLD** water, then add to sauce pan. Cook over medium-high heat, stirring constantly, until thickened. If gravy doesn't thicken sufficiently, add ½ tablespoon cornstach dissolved in ¼ cup **COLD** water and continue to cook and stir. Serve with **1976-BICENTINIAL TURKEY DRESSING** (page 11).

Use remainder of fat-free broth for liquid in **1976-BICENTENNIAL TURKEY DRESSING.** Or, refrigerate liquid overnight, remove solidified fat, and place broth in plastic carton and freeze for future use. Prepare this gravy when roasting turkey without apple–cider basting.

TURKEY HASH

1 cup fat-free turkey broth (see **TURKEY GIBBLET GRAVY**—page 72)
1 medium onion finely chopped
2 cups ½-inch chunks of dark meat from roast turkey
6 medium mushrooms sliced ⅛-inch thick
1 tablespoon soy sauce
1 tablespoon Worcestershire® sauce
½ tablespoon beef bouillon
1 teaspoon tarragon
½ teaspoon monosodium glutamate
1½ tablespoons corn starch
1 tablespoon canola oil

In sauce pan, saute onion and mushrooms in oil until onion is translucent and limp. Add broth, turkey, sauces, and spices, and heat to low boil. Dissolve corn starch in ¼ cup **COLD** water and add to material in sauce pan. Continue cooking over medium-high heat stirring constantly until thick and bubbly. Serve over hard toast or with rice or mashed potatoes.

TURKEYBURGERS

3 pounds ground turkey
1 tablespoon thyme
1 tablespoon basil
1 tablespoon garlic powder
1 tablespoon monosodium glutamate
1 tablespoon beef bouillon

1 tablespoon Worcestershire® sauce
1½ teaspoons black pepper
1 8- by 8-inch piece of ⅜-inch exterior plywood
Wax paper
Nonstick spray oil
No. 100 sandpaper

Mix meat, spices, and seasonings thoroughly; make sure that the spices are evenly distributed through the meat.

With a scroll-saw, cut a 5½-inch-diameter hole in the exact center of the plywood. Sand rough edges. Spray edges of hole with nonstick oil. Place plywood with hole on one end of a 12-inch-long piece of wax paper. With fork, fill hole with meat mixture level with plywood. Remove plywood, fold wax paper over meat. Repeat until all meat is made into patties; stack wax-paper-wrapped patties then seal in plastic bag. Freeze. Makes 10–12 patties.

To cook burgers, remove wax paper and place frozen patties on broiler pan sprayed with nonstick oil. Adjust oven rack so that burgers are about 3–4 inches below broiler. Broil on "high" for about 7 minutes, turn patties and broil for about 2½ minutes longer. Serve on large sesame-seed bun with condiments and relishes commonly used with hamburgers.

Plywood mold may be washed, dried, and reused. Spices and seasonings may be adjusted to personal tastes.

TURKEY SAUSAGE

1½ pounds ground turkey
1 tablespoon ground sage
1 tablespoon "smoke" salt
2 tablespoon poultry seasoning
No. 100 sandpaper

1 teaspoon black pepper
1 5- by 5-inch piece of 3/8-inch exterior plywood
Wax paper
Nonstick spray oil

Mix spices and seasonings into meat thoroughly; make sure that spices are distributed evenly throughout meat.

With a scroll-saw, cut a 3¼-inch-diameter hole in the exact center of the plywood. Sand rough edges. Spray edges of hole with nonstick oil. Place plywood on 1 end of a 6-inch wide strip of 12-inch wax paper. With a fork, fill hole in plywood with meat mixture level with plywood. Remove plywood, fold wax paper over pattie, and stack patties. Seal patties in plastic bag and freeze.

To cook sausages, remove wax paper and place frozen patties on broiler pan sprayed with nonstick spray oil. Adjust oven rack so that patties are about 3–4 inches below broiler. Broil on "high" for about 7 minutes; turn and broil 2½ minutes longer. Sausages also may be cooked in cast-iron frying pan sprayed with nonstick oil; turn burner to medium and cook until sausage is cooked through. Serve as breakfast meat with waffles, pancakes, or omlets.

Plywood mold may be washed, dried, and reused. Spices and seasonings may be adjusted to personal tastes.

A story goes with the previous 2 recipes. For Christmas, 1½ months after we married, my new spouse and I made my mother-in-law, who was spending the holidays with us, a form for sausage and hamburgers. We made the combination form in the shape of the numeral "8" with the smaller sausage form on top. Upon opening the package, my mother-in-law asked "what is it?" My wife and I in unison said "It's an 8." Then, my wife indicated the utility of the device and her mother responded that indeed it might be useful. I chimed in with "next year I will make a '7' for you." My mother-in-law responded with "Oh, that will be nice," never recognizing the pun.

SLOPPY TOMS

1¼ pounds ground turkey
1 medium onion
10 medium mushrooms
½ bell pepper
1–2 tablespoons canola oil
1 teaspoon thyme

1 teaspoon sweet basil
1 teaspoon monosodium glutamate
1 teaspoon salt
1 8-ounce can tomato sauce
4 large hamburger buns with sesame seeds

Wash and finely chop onion, mushrooms, and bell pepper. In Dutch oven over medium-high heat, saute vegetables with ¼ of oil until onion is limp and translucent. Remove from Dutch oven. Add remaining oil and ground turkey to Dutch oven; stir continuously until meat is browned and no water remains in bottom of Dutch oven. Add spices and sauted vegetables and stir, then add tomato sauce and mix thoroughly. Warm buns by placing them in plastic bag in microwave for 30 seconds. Place ¼ of meat-vegetable mixture on each bun. Serve with oven French fries.

This is adapted from a recipe for Sloppy Joes, but in view that I use ground turkey instead of ground beef, I consider the name **SLOPPY TOMS** more appropriate.

UNSTUFFED PEPPERS

1 pound ground turkey
1 cup **STEAMED RICE** (page 25)
1 medium onion
2–3 large cloves garlic
3 medium tomatoes
4 large mushrooms
2 large green peppers
1 teaspoon monosodium glutamate

½ teaspoon thyme
½ teaspoon basil
1 teaspoon salt
¼ teaspoon black pepper
1 tablespoon Worcestershire® sauce
2 teaspoons beef bouillon
2–3 tablespoons canola oil
Nonstick spray oil

Peel tomatoes, garlic, and onion; wash mushrooms; wash and remove tops, seeds, and membranes from peppers. (To peel tomatoes, place in mixing bowl and cover with boiling water. Fill bowl with cold water as soon as skin splits; skin will slip from tomato easily.) Chop vegetables, then saute in 1–1½ tablespoons oil in Dutch oven or large cast-iron skillet over medium high heat; stir constantly until most of liquid has evaporated. Remove from skillet, rinse skillet, and saute meat in remaining oil, stirring constantly to break meat into small crumbles. Meat will exude considerable water; add bouillon and Worcestershire® sauce at this point and continue stirring until almost all water evaporates. Add vegetables, spices, and seasonings to meat and mix thoroughly. Place ¼ of mixture in each of 4 oven-safe casseroles sprayed with nonstick oil; pack gently. Bake for 20 minutes at 350°F. Serve with mashed potatoes. (Yes, I know rice and potatoes are a lot of starch, but the dishes go well together.)

STUFFED PEPPERS

Prepare as for **UNSTUFFED PEPPERS** except do not chop peppers. Instead, increase number of peppers to 4 (pick square-sided and flat-bottomed peppers if possible) and after removing tops, membranes, and seeds steam them for 10 minutes. Fill peppers with meat-rice-vegetable mixture and place them upright in high-sided baking dish sprayed lightly with nonstick spray oil. Bake for 20 minutes at 350°F.

COTTAGE PIE

1½ pounds ground turkey
2 medium onions
3 medium carrots
2 large stalks celery
2 cloves garlic
1 tablespoon chili powder
½ teaspoon cummin

1 tablespoon cilantro
½ teaspoon oregano
1 teaspoon beef bouillon
dash freshly ground black pepper
1 pint or 1 can Roma tomatoes
Nonstick spray oil
1 crust (recipe follows)

Spray Dutch oven with nonstick oil; saute ground turkey at medium or medium-high heat until the moisture is gone. Remove meat from Dutch oven, wipe oven, and spray with oil again. Saute onions, celery, carrots, and garlic until onions are translucent. Add spices, meat, and tomatoes, and continue cooking at medium heat until reduced by ⅓; stir frequently. Pour mixture into 9- by 9-inch glass baking dish and cover with crust.

COTTAGE PIE CRUST

¼ cup yellow corn meal
⅓+ cup flour
1 teaspoon baking powder
¼ teaspoon salt

¼ teaspoon cayenne pepper
1 egg white
½ tablespoon egg substitute (Eggbeaters®)
¼ cup milk

Mix dry ingredients then add liquids and mix thoroughly. Pour over meat mixture and bake 350°F for 25 minutes.

MEATPIE

1 box hot roll mix
1¼ cups hot water
2 tablespoons olive oil
2 pounds low-fat ground turkey
2 tablespoons Worcestershire® sauce

2 tablespoons dried parsley
1 tablespoon dried thyme
1 tablespoon dried sweet basil
¼ pound Tillamook® cheddar cheese
Nonstick spray oil

Mix contents of roll mix box and yeast packet in large bowl. Add hot water and olive oil. Stir until dough forms; turn out dough onto lighly floured bread board and knead for 5 minutes. Divide dough into 8 pieces. Let dough rest for 10 minutes.

Grind herbs with mortar and pestle and mix with meat thoroughly. With fork, force ½ pound of meat into 5½-inch-diameter by ⅜-inch-thick **TURKEYBURGER** mold (page 73) sprayed with nonstick oil. Spray broiler pan with nonstick spray oil. Arrange the 4 meat patties on broiler pan and broil on top rack about 7 minutes on first side and about 2 minutes on second side. Remove from beneath broiler and cut each patty in half.

On lightly floured bread board, roll each piece of dough into a 6-inch circle. Place half a meat patty on each circle, sprinkle with ½-ounce cheese, and fold dough over to form a half circle. Press edges with fork to seal; prick dough with fork to allow steam to escape. Place meat pies on cookie sheet sprayed with nonstick oil and bake in preheated 425°F oven for 12–15 minutes. Serve warm or place in plastic bag and freeze; reheat in microwave.

With tossed salad, meatpies make a nice lunch.

MEAT LOAF/MEAT BALLS

2 pounds ground turkey
1 medium onion
2 large cloves of garlic
½ cup 1% milk
2 tablespoons Worcestershire® sauce
2 tablespoons soy sauce
4 egg whites
2 tablespoons parsley flakes

1 tablespoon garlic powder
1 teaspoon thyme
1 teaspoon basil
1 teaspoon salt
1 teaspooon monosodium glutamate
½ teaspoon freshly ground black pepper
2–2½ cups dry bread crumbs
Nonstick spray oil

Remove outer layer and root nodes from onion and garlic. Place onion, garlic, spices, and liquid ingredients in blender and puree. Pour puree over ground turkey and mix thoroughly with fork. Add bread crumbs about ½ cup at a time and mix; continue until mixture has a firm, but not pasty texture. For meat loaf, form into loaves with rubber spatula in glass baking dishes sprayed with nonstick oil. Bake loaves at 350°F for 45 minutes. For meat balls, roll 2-tablespoon amounts into balls; set balls on wax paper. Spray large cast-iron skillet with nonstick oil and brown balls over medium heat. Recipe makes about 100 meat balls, 2 meat loaves, or 1 meat loaf and about 50 meat balls.

To preserve meatballs, freeze on cookie sheet then store in plastic bags. Add to spaghetti sauce during last 30 minutes of cooking. To perserve meat loaves, wrap in wax paper, place in plastic bags, and freeze.

MEAT LOAF, TOO

1½ pounds ground turkey
1 medium onion
4–5 cloves garlic
1 tablespoon Worcestershire® sauce
1 tablespoon soy sauce
2 egg whites
1 tablespoon parsley flakes

1 tablespoon garlic powder
1 teaspoon thyme
1 teaspoon basil
2 tablespoons catsup
½ teaspoon freshly ground black pepper
¼–½ cup bread crumbs
Nonstick spray oil

Remove outer layer and root nodes from onion and garlic; chop garlic finely. Place oninon, garlic, spices, egg whites, soy sauce, catsup, and Worcestirshire® sauce in blender and puree. Pour puree over ground turkey and mix thoroughly with fork. Add bread crumbs ¼ cup at a time and mix; continue until mixture has a firm texture. Spray glass baking dish with nonstick spray oil. Form turkey mixture into loaf with rubber spatula in dish. Cover with plastic wrap and refrigerate overnight to allow melding of spices. Bake in 350°F oven for 65 minutes.

For an interesting and tasty variation, add ¼ cup Parmesan cheese to the mixture.

This recipe also can be used for meat balls. See previous recipe for cooking instructions.

MEAT–LOAF ROLL

MEAT LOAF

½ pound 9%-fat ground sirloin
1 pound ground turkey
2 egg whites
⅓ cup egg substitute (Eggbeaters®)
½ cup 1% milk
½ teaspoon basil
½ teaspoon garlic powder
1½ teaspoons salt
1 cup bread crumbs

1 teaspoon ground sage
1 teaspoon "smoke" salt
2 teaspoons poultry seasoning
½ teaspoon black pepper
½ teaspoon thyme
¼ teaspoon tarragon
½ teaspoon onion powder
½ teaspoon monosodium glutamate

Mix 5 five items in left column with mixer at low speed until homogeneous; add spices and mix thoroughly. Remove from mixer and add bread crumbs. Mix with rubber spatula. Cover and refrigerate several hours or overnight.

Spray 12- by 16-inch piece of aluminum foil with nonstick spray oil. Spread meat mixture over 12- by 12-inch area about ½-inch thick. Hold for stuffing.

STUFFING

1–2 cloves garlic
2 tablespoons canola oil
1½ cups fresh tomatoes skinned and chopped
    or 1½ cups canned Roma tomatoes drained
¼ teaspoon salt
¼ teaspoon oregano
6 ounces Tillamook® cheddar cheese grated

1 bay leaf
1 cup finely chopped onion
½ cup finely chopped bell pepper
2 cups mushrooms sliced
½ teaspoon thyme
¼ teaspoon monosodium glutamate

Saute garlic and bay leaf in oil in Dutch oven until garlic is translucent. Add remaining items except cheese and continue to saute until most liquid is evaporated. Remove bay leaf and discard.

Spread stuffing in center of meatloaf material; cover with grated cheddar cheese. Fold edges of meat loaf over stuffing and overlap about 1 inch. Close ends and overlapped edges of meat loaf to enclose stuffing completely. Spray broiling rack with nonstick spray oil. Leave rack on broiling pan. With 1 person holding each end of aluminum foil, gently flip meat–loaf roll upside down onto broiling rack. Bake at 350°F for 45 minutes. Serve with **MASHED POTATOES** (page 30) or **MACARONI AND CHEESE** (page 30) and steamed broccoli or green peas.

A friend from Australia, claimed that my meat–loaf roll was the first dish that he had eaten during his year-long sabbatical in North America that "had a bit of taste." I took that as the finest compliment ever extended to my cooking!

PRESSURE-COOKER STEW

1½ pounds turkey tenders cut into 1-inch cubes
1 large onion
10 medium mushrooms cut into quarters
2–3 large carrots cut into 1-inch pieces
2–3 potatoes peeled and cut into 1½-inch chunks
1 large green pepper
½ tablespoon beef bouillon
2–3 tablespoons soy sauce

2 tablespoons canola oil
1½ cups water
1½ tablespoons corn starch
¼ cup cold water
1 teaspoon thyme
1 teaspoon basil
¼ teaspoon black pepper

In bottom of pressure cooker, saute meat in oil. Add water, soy sauce, and bouillon; pressure cook at 15 pounds for 7 minutes. Remove pressure by placing cooker under cold water. Layer onions, carrots, peppers, potatoes, and mushrooms on top of meat in that order. Raise pressure to 15 pounds and cook for 4 minutes. Remove pressure by placing cooker under cold water. Mix corn starch in **COLD** water and add to meat and vegetables; thicken by cooking over medium heat, stirring constantly (requires 1–2 minutes). Add spices. Serve in bowl accompanied by a large chunk of **SOURDOUGH FRENCH BREAD** (page 20). This is a hearty winter meal that is quick to prepare and will warm you all the way to the tip of your toes.

Back in the days when I ate beef, I cut the center eye of a blade-cut pot roast into cubes; it was cheap and flavorful meat. However, the mock-beef stew made with turkey tenders is equally as good.

PRESSURE-COOKER STEW, TOO

1½ pounds turkey tenders

1 tablespoon canola oil

2 8-inch carrots

2 medium potatoes

4 broccoli stalks (peeled)

5 medium mushrooms (quartered)

2 stalks celery

1 large onion

3 cloves garlic

2½ cups water (or 1 cup cold beer & 1½ cups water)

3 tablespoons cornstarch

1 teaspoon sweet basil

1 teaspoon thyme

¼ teaspoon freshly ground black pepper

1 teaspoon monosodium glutamate

1 tablespoon beef bouillon

1 tablespoon soy sauce

1 tablespoon Worcestershire® sauce

1 teaspoon red wine vinegar

Trim fat and tendons from turkey and cut into ¾–1-inch cubes. Place oil and turkey in bottom of 3-quart pressure cooker over medium high heat stirring constantly until meat turns whitish. Add 1½ cups water, cover with pressure lid, increase heat to high, raise pressure to 15 pounds; reduce temperature to maintain even pressure and cook for 7 minutes.

While meat cooks, clean vegetables and cut into ¾-inch chunks (except garlic which should be pressed or finely chopped). Grind dry spices with monosodium glutamate with mortar and pestle. Mix bouillon, sauces, vinegar, and cornstarch with 1 cup cold water (or beer).

Remove cooker from heat and cool under cold running water until pressure is gone. Remove lid, add vegetables, replace lid, and return to high heat until pressure returns to 15 pounds; reduce temperature to maintain even pressure and cook for 4 minutes ONLY. Remove from heat, reduce pressure to zero, remove lid, and return to medium heat. Mix cornstarch in ¼ cup **COLD** water. Add spices and cornstarch mixture (make sure to stir well just before adding to cooker) and cook (without lid) until mixture thickens. Makes 4 large servings. Serve with **SOURDOUGH BAKING POWDER BISCUITS** (page 21). This makes a great low-cholesterol, low-fat supper for a cold winter night. A spoonful of strawberry jam on 1 last biscuit is the perfect dessert.

FISH AND OTHER SEA FOODS

My father took me fishing on Salt Fork River when I was not yet 4 years old. And, that afternoon, I caught my first fish, a 4-inch-long green sunfish. I became an avid fisherman, first with a cane pole, then a fly rod, and finally a spinning rod. During college days, I found 20 minutes of fly casting for bass in the University Pond a diversion that maintained a sembalance of sanity when pressured by courses, prelims, research, and other hurdles—even when no fish were caught.

Upon obtaining a new professorship in an entirely new geographic region with a totally different fauna (including fish), I was indoctorinated by colleagues to various outdoor sports that included fishing for salmon, steelhead, trout, perch, flounder, and rockfish in addition to freshwater species with which I was already accustomed. Wow! Eight–10-pound steelhead, 18–25-pound salmon, 12–16-inch trout, and unlimited catches of bottomfish. To these catches were added digging for softshell and long-neck clams, running crab pots, and netting crayfish.

For nearly 20 years I wallowed in this utopia. I accumulated boats, motors, nets, rods, reels, boots, float coats, and a plethora of smaller gear. Then, as suddenly as it began when I was 4 years old, it was over. Populations of fishes declined, populations of fishermen exploded, and regulations became more and more restrictive—and, in many instances, exasperatingly complex. It wasn't fun anymore. I quit!

Would you believe, during most of my fishing days, I didn't care much for the fish that I brought home even though my catches were fresher and cleaner than anything available in any grocery or fish market. At least part of my lack of enthusiasm for fish was in the way that they were prepared. In my household, white-meated fish were fried and salmon and steelhead were poached or baked. I like poached or baked salmon and steelhead, but I fairly frequently filled or got close to filling my 20-fish annual limit—that's more poached and baked fish than I want to think about. So, it wasn't until after my emancipation when I began to try other ways of preparing fish that I began to enjoy it. I won't go into details, but a few of my attempts were utter disasters. Some of my better recipes follow:

GRILLED SNAPPER

2 fresh snapper (rockfish) fillets (about ½ pound each)
2–3 tablespoons soy sauce
1–2 tablespoons lemon juice
½ teaspoon each dried tarragon and cilintro (ground with mortar and pestle)
½ teaspoon ground paprika
1 teaspoon powdered garlic
1 tablespoon sesame oil
Nonstick spray oil

Remove rib bones from snapper fillets and place in 9- by 13-inch glass baking dish. Spinkle with lemon juice and soy sauce, turn fillets to coat evenly. Place fillets in refrigerator for 30 minutes or longer, turn fillets once. Heat griddle on medium for 10 minutes; turn griddle to heat evenly if different-sized burners are used. Spray griddle with nonstick oil and sprinkle with sesame oil. Sprinkle inside of fillets with ½ of ground spices. Place spice-side down on griddle when oil begins to turn brown. Sprinkle other side of fillets with remaining spices. Turn fillets with 2 pancake turners. Remove and serve when flesh is opaque and begins to flake apart—about 10 minutes cooking time. Serves 2. Excellent with **RICE PILAF** (pages 25–26) and a steamed vegetable. Serve with **TARTAR SAUCE** (page 107). Marinating fillets gives time to feed the dogs and watch the evening news.

GRILLED SNAPPER

SNAPPER-N-SPUDS

3–4 medium potatoes
1¼–1½ pounds snapper fillets (about ¾-inch thick)
4 tablespoons olive oil
1½ tablespoons dried parsley

Peel potatoes and slice them about ⅛–¼-inch-thick cross-wise of their long axis. Place them in a 9- by 13-inch glass baking dish, add 2½ tablespoons of oil, and half of the parsley. Mix thoroughly and bake uncovered at 400°F for 40 minutes.

Remove rib bones from snapper fillets. Coat fillets with remaining oil and parsley. Place on top of cooked potatoes and return to 400°F oven for about 20 minutes. Dish is done when fish begins to flake apart when the thickest part is touched with a fork. Serve with **TARTAR SAUCE** (page 107).

OVEN-FRIED FISH FOR TWO

2 fillets of snapper or other bottomfish (about ⅓-pound each)
2 tablespoons eggs substitute (Eggbeaters®)
3 cups bread crumbs spread in 1-inch layer on wax paper
1–2 tablespoon canola oil
1 tablespoon garlic powder
1 tablespoon lemon juice
¼ teaspoon tarragon (ground finely in mortar and pestle)
Nonstick spray oil

Remove ribs from filets and dip fillets in egg substitute 1 at a time. Place fillet on bread crumbs and cover with bread crumbs. Press bread crumbs into fillet with palm of hand. Shake fillet gently to remove excess bread crumbs. Place in 9- by 13-inch baking dish sprayed with nonstick oil. Sprinkle fish with lemon juice, oil, garlic powder, and tarragon. Bake in 500°F oven for 12 minutes. Return unused bread crumbs to container for future use. Serve with **TARTAR SAUCE** (page 107).

FISH FROMAGE

¾–1 pound snapper (rockfish) fillets
1 medium onion (chopped finely)
¼ pound Tillamook® cheddar cheese (grated)
½ cup 1% milk
2 teaspoons Worcestershire® sauce
½ teaspoon salt
1 teaspoon grey poupon mustard
½ teaspoon rosemary
½ teaspoon sweet basil
Nonstick spray oil

Remove ribs from fish fillets. Spread evenly in 9- by 9-inch baking dish that has been sprayed with nonstick oil. Sprinkle chopped onion and grate cheese evenly over fish. Mix milk, salt, mustard, and Worchestershire sauce; pour over fish. Grind rosemary and basil in mortar and pestle; sprinkle over fish. Bake uncovered in 450°F oven for 25–30 minutes.

Serve with pancake turner. This is a spicy dish that goes well with **CREAMED NEW POTATOES** (page 28) and steamed green peas.

CITRUS SNAPPER

2 large fillets of red snapper, about 1½ pounds total.
¼ cup frozen orange-juice concentrate
2 tablespoons lemon juice
2 tablespoons water
1 tablespoon canola oil
¼ teaspoon dill
½ cup cold water
1 tablespoon corn starch
Aluminum foil
Nonstick spray oil

Remove rib bones for fish and place in 9- by 13-inch baking dish sprayed with nonstick oil. Mix orange-juice concentrate, lemon juice, 2 tablespoons water, oil, and dill. Pour over fish and marinate overnight in refrigerator; turn fish seveal times. Drain fish, but save marinade. Spray baking dish with nonstick oil, add fish, cover with foil, and bake for 35 minutes in 350°F oven. Combine marinade and liquid from fish; add cornstarch dissolved in cold water. Cook over medium heat until lightly thickened. Pour over fish. Serve with **STEAMED RICE** (page 25).

LIMON SNAPPER

2 medium fillets of red snapper (total weight about ¾ pound)
2 ripe limes
1½ tablespoons canola oil

Remove rib bones from fillets. Arrange fillets in 9- by 13-inch baking dish and cover with juice of the 2 limes; turn several times to insure that fillets are covered with lime juice. Cover with plastic wrap and refrigerate; turn fillets at hourly intervals for 4 hours. Add oil and coat thoroughly. Bake uncovered at 400°F for 20–25 minutes depending on thickness of fillets.

CURRIED SNAPPER

2 large fillets of snapper (about ½ pound each)
2–3 tablespoons lemon juice or lime juice
1 teaspoon curry powder
1 teaspoon garlic powder
1 teaspoon onion powder
1 teaspoon monosodium glutamate
2 tablespoons sesame oil
2–3 tablespoons plain yogurt
Nonstick spray oil

Remove rib bones from fillets. Place fillets in baking dish and coat both sides with lemon or lime juice; refrigerate for 1–2 hours. Mix spices in old spice jar with perforated cap. Spray griddle with nonstick oil and heat over medium or medium low burners; add sesame oil and spread evenly. Sprinkle 1 side of fillets with ½ of spices. Place fillets on griddle spice-side down. Sprinkle other side of fillets with remaining spices. Use 2 pancake turners to turn. Cook until thickest part of fish just begins to flake. Serve with a dolop of yogurt spread over each fillet.

POACHED FLOUNDER WITH SAUTED CABBAGE AND CHEESE SAUCE

POACHED FLOUNDER

1 pound flounder fillets
1 medium onion sliced and separated into rings
1 tablespoon lemon juice
1 clove garlic chopped finely
½ teaspoon salt
¼ teaspoon pepper
¼ cup water

Place flounder in 9- by 13-inch baking dish; add onion rings and garlic; mix water, lemon juice, salt and pepper and pour over fish. Cover dish with foil and poach in 350°F oven for about 15–16 minutes. Fish should flake easily.

SAUTED CABBAGE

½ medium head cabbage shredded
¼ cup white wine (French Colombard is a nice choice)
½ tablespoons canola oil
¼ teaspoon salt

While flounder poaches, add oil to cast-iron skillet over medium heat, then add cabbage, wine, and sprinkle with salt. Cover and cook for 5–6 minutes, stirring occasionally; remove cover and cook for 5–6 additional minutes. Cabbage should be tender but still crisp.

Transfer cabbage to fish-shaped baking dish or 9- by 13-inch baking dish. Carefully transfer fish to top of cabbage with 2 pancake turners.

CHEESE SAUCE

1 tablespoon canola oil
¼ cup flour
½ teaspoon salt
1½ cups 1% milk
¼ cup poaching liquid reserved from fish
1 cup shredded low-fat Swiss cheese

While flounder poaches and cabbage sautes, place oil in saucepan over medium heat, add flour and stir. Add milk and poaching liquid and stir constantly with wire whisk. Add salt and ½ of the cheese. Continue stirring until sauce thickens. Pour over fish and cabbage. Top with remaining cheese. Place under broiler until cheese sauce is lightly browned-about 2–3 minutes. Sole may be substituted for flounder, but it is not as strongly flavored as flounder. Serve with **STEAMED RICE** (page 25).

The poached flounder dish requires that components be prepared in advance and that cooking of the 3 elements be coordinated precisely. With a bit of practice this is a dish that will impress the boss, girl friend, or mother-in-law with both your organization and culinary skills. Unfortunately, preparation leaves the kitchen quite a mess, with no time to hide any of it in the dishwasher.

FLOUNDER IN BEER BATTER

1 pound flounder fillets
1 cup warm beer
1 cup flour
½ teaspoon salt
1 tablespoon dry yeast
1–2 pints canola oil

Mix yeast, flour, and salt with ½ cup beer; stir until smooth. Add remainder of beer and stir until smooth again. Let batter stand in warm place for 30 minutes. Beat batter again. Remove rib bones from flounder and cut fish into 1-inch cubes. Dip pieces of fish into batter and deep fry in oil at 355°F.

Other fish such as ling cod, snapper, or ocean perch can be substituted for flounder. Also, small chunks of chicken can be dipped into the batter and fried in the same manner as fish. This is NOT a dish recommended for those on a restricted-fat diet. I have not prepared this dish in years, but savor the memory of its odor and taste, and the accolades from those to whom I served it.

BAKED LING COD WITH MUSHROOM SAUCE

2 fillets of ling cod about 6–8 ounces each
¼ pound mushrooms (sliced)
1 small onion (chopped)
2 tablespoons canola oil
2 tablespoons flour
1 cup 1% milk
3 tablespoons white wine (French Colombard is a nice choice)
1 tablespoon Worcestershire® sauce
¼ cup grated Parmesan cheese
⅛ teaspoon pepper
½ teaspoon salt
¾ teaspoon tarragon
1 tablespoon parsley (chopped)
Nonstick spray oil

Remove ribs from fish and put fish in 9- by 9-inch baking dish sprayed with nonstick oil. Saute mushrooms and onion in 1 tablespoon of oil until onions are transparent and mushrooms are limp. Reduce heat and add remaining oil and flour; mix in milk, then add wine, spices, salt, and cheese. Stir until sauce thickens. Pour sauce over fish and bake uncovered in 350°F oven for 30 minutes. Sprinkle with chopped parsley.

Snapper (rockfish) can be substituted for the ling cod with good success. This is a low-fat dish that is filling; eat 1 of these fillets and you will know that you have had dinner.

PERCH AND VEGETABLES

¾ pound ocean perch fillets
12 snowpeas
4 medium carrots (sliced thinly lengthwise)
1 small zucchini unpealed (sliced crosswise)
1 small onion (sliced and separated into rings)
½ teaspoon salt

⅛ teaspoon pepper
½ teaspoon tarragon
2 tablespoons lemon juice
¼ cup grated Parmesan cheese
Aluminum foil
Nonstick spray oil

Spray 9- by 9-inch baking dish with nonstick spray oil. Remove rib bones from fillets and spread fish evenly over dish. Sprinkle with lemon juice. Add vegetables, salt, pepper, and tarragon. Cover with foil and bake in 350°F oven for 30 minutes. Sprinkle with Parmesan cheese before serving.

This is a easy way to fix meat and vegetables at the same time. Serve with steamed rice. As cooking time for the fish and vegetables, and the rice is about the same, this gives about 20 minutes to give the dogs a walk while dinner cooks—or you can be a couch potato and watch the evening news.

My spouse, who claims to have forgotten everything she ever knew about cooking when she married me, fixed this dish for dinner the day that I came home from the hospital after major surgery. Maybe going without food other than liquids for 4–5 days and a bland hospital diet for the rest of the week had something to do with it, but that meal was the best food I've ever eaten. Don't wait until after a week-long stay in the hospital to try this simple dish!

SWEET-AND-SOUR PERCH

4 fillets live-bearing perch, about ¼ pound each
1–2 tablespoons cornstarch
1 teaspoon salt
2–3 tablespoons canola oil
¼ cup sugar
⅓ cup apple-cider vinegar
3 tablespoons soy sauce
3 tablespoons catsup
Nonstick spray oil

Place cornstarch and salt in plastic bag. Remove bones from fish. Shake each fillet in cornstarch-salt mixture separately. Heat oil in large skillet over medium heat until it just begins to smoke. Fry fish about 2½ minutes on each side (use mesh spatter guard to reduce mess). Remove from heat to plate with double layer of paper towels; blot fish on both sides. Place fillets in 9- by 13-inch baking dish sprayed with nonstick oil.

Mix sugar, vinegar, soy sauce and catsup in small glass dish; cover with plastic wrap. Heat in microwave on high 1 minute; stir and heat 1 additional minute. Cover fillets with sauce. Bake at 350°F for 15 minutes. Serve with rice and peas for a really tasty main course. Serves 2. Substituting small fillets of snapper for perch in the recipe is a satisfactory alternative.

FRIED PERCH

1 pound ocean perch fillets
2 tablespoons egg substitute (Eggbeaters®)
½ cup white cornmeal
3–4 tablespoons canola or olive oil

Remove bones from perch fillets. Coat fillets with egg substitute then press into cornmeal spread on wax paper; coat both sides of fish. Heat ½ of oil in large skillet over medium heat. Place fish in skillet; add oil as needed. Fry until crisp and slightly brown on both sides. Blot with paper towels to remove excess oil. Serve with **TARTAR SAUCE** (page 107).

Catfish prepared this way and fried in ½-inch of lard was the only way that I knew that fish could be prepared until I joined the Navy. No wonder I didn't like fish as a youngster! However, a delicately flavored fish (such as the live-bearing perch that occurs along the Pacific Coast) covered with white cornmeal and fried in a light oil has a delicious crunchy texture and a nutty flavor. It goes well with mashed or scalloped potatoes and spinach or other green vegetable. This sounds so good that I think that that is what I will fix tonight.

PERCH IN CREAM SAUCE

1 pound ocean perch fillets
2 tablespoons soy sauce
1 tablespoon lemon juice
1 tablespoon sesame oil
Nonstick spray oil

Clean fish, remove bones, and marinate in soy sauce and lemon juice for 30 minutes to 1 hour. Heat griddle over medium heat for 15 minutes. Spray with nonstick oil and add sesame oil. Grill fish 5–6 minutes on each side or until it commences to flake.

CREAM SAUCE FOR PERCH

¼ cup flour
2 tablespoons canola oil
½ tablespoon chicken boullion
1 cup chicken broth
1 cup milk

¼ cup grated Parmesan cheese
½ teaspoon tarragon
½ teaspoon cilantro
⅛ teaspoon black pepper

Warm oil over medium heat. Stir in flour and mix thoroughly. Add milk and chicken broth. Raise heat to medium high and stir continuously with wisk. Add other ingredients and continue to stir until sauce thickens. Pour over grilled fish. Garnish with chopped chives or green onions. Serve with **STEAMED RICE** (page 25) or **FETTUCINI** (page 32) and green vegetable. Red snapper can be substituted for ocean perch, but be sure to pick small fillets.

SOLE AND SPINACH

1 pound fillets of sole
1 pound fresh spinach leaves
½ teaspoon salt
Aluminum foil
Nonstick spray oil

Spray 9- by 9-inch baking dish with nonstick oil. Wash spinach leaves and shake to remove excess water. Add about half of the spinach leaves to the baking dish. Arrange fillets of sole evenly over spinach. Sprinkle with salt. Cover with remaining spinach. Press to flatten spinach even with top of baking dish. Spray inside of foil used to cover dish with nonstick oil. Bake 30 minutes at 350°F. Remove with pancake turner. Squeeze gently between 2 pancake turners to remove excess moisture before placing on plate. Serve with steamed rice, **CREAMED NEW POTATOES** (page 28) or a pan of fresh-baked **CORNBREAD** (page 10). This sounds awful even to someone who likes spinach, but it is surprisingly tasty.

SOLE ITALIANO

6 fillets of Dover sole (about ½ pound)
1 16-ounce can tomato sauce
1 tablespoon Worchestershire® sauce
1 tablespoon olive oil
6 medium mushrooms
1 small onion

1 clove garlic
1 tablespoon oregano
1 teaspoon thyme
6 wooden toothpicks
Nonstick spray oil

Remove rib bones from fish. Roll each fillet and secure with toothpick. Spray 5- by 6½-inch baking dish with nonstick spray oil. Heat oil over medium high heat; saute sliced onion, mushrooms, and chopped garlic until onion is limp and mushrooms are softened. Add tomato sauce, Worchestershire sauce, and spices; stir. Place fish in dish and cover with mixture of tomato sauce, mushrooms, and herbs. Make sure that toothpicks are covered with tomato sauce, otherwise they burn. Bake at 350°F for 20 minutes. Serve over spaghetti.

SOLE AND VEGGIES

12 fillets of sole (about 1½ pounds)
2 medium carrots
4 medium mushrooms
½ medium onion
10 green beans
1 small zucchini
1 small green pepper

1 tablespoon sesame oil
2 tablespoons lemon juice
1 teaspoon monosodium glutamate (optional)
salt and pepper to taste
Aluminum foil
Nonstick spray oil

Wash vegetables; cut carrots and pepper into matchstick-size pieces, slice mushrooms and zucchini ⅛-inch thick, cut beans in ½-inch lengths, and chop onion finely. Stir-fry vegetables in sesame oil in wok first sprayed with nonstick oil. Spray 8- by 8-inch pyrex baking dish with nonstick oil. Line bottom of baking dish with 4 fillets then add vegetables and follow by alternating 2 layers of fillets. Sprinkle with lemon juice, monosodium glutamate, salt and pepper; cover with foil and bake at 350°F for 25 minutes. Serve with **STEAMED RICE** (page 25) or a pasta dish. Serves 2 with enough left over for 1 lunch the following day.

SOLE FOOD

9–10 fillets of Dover sole
½ cup finely chopped onion
8 medium mushrooms sliced
½ cup finely chopped broccoli head

3 medium asparagus spears diced
1 medium carrot grated
Aluminum foil
Nonstick spray oil

Spray 9- by 9-inch baking dish with nonstick oil. Distribute ½ the onion over bottom of dish followed by a layer consisting of ½ the sole. Distribute remaining vegetables evenly over bottom layer of sole and follow with another layer of sole. Cover with aluminum foil and bake at 350°F for 30 minutes. Remove foil, cover fish with sauce (recipe follows), sprinkle lightly with paprika, and bake an additional 5 minutes at 400°F.

SAUCE FOR SOLE

¼ cup flour
2 tablespoons canola oil
1¼ cups 1% milk
1 teaspoon chicken bouillon
½ teaspoon monosodium glutamate

¼ teaspoon tarragon
¼ teaspoon chervil
½ teaspoon salt
¼ cup Parmesan cheese

Warm oil, add flour, and mix thoroughly with wisk. Raise temperature to medium high, add milk, bouillon, spices, and salt. Continue to stir with wisk until mixture commences to thicken. Add Parmesan cheese and stir until smooth.

POACHED SALMON OR STEELHEAD

6-inch long chunk from the midsection of 7–8 pound fish
1 thinly-sliced lemon
1 small onion sliced
1 bay leaf
2 sprigs parsley
8–10 peppercorns
4 quarts water
18-inch long piece of cheese cloth
2 pincer-type wooden clothes pins

Wash fish and remove any kidney that remains against the spine. Bring water, lemon juice, onion, and bay leaf to a boil. Wrap fish in several layers of cheese cloth leaving 5–6 inches free at each end; twist ends of cheese cloth. Immerse fish in water. Cover and attach clothes pins to twisted cheese cloth so that fish is suspended in the water. Simmer 1 hour—DO NOT BOIL. Lift fish from water by twisted ends of cheese cloth.

Remove skin, then remove flesh from bones. Serve in chunks alone, with **EGG SAUCE** (described below), or use in **LEFT-OVER SALMON LOAF** (page 94), **SALMON SALAD** (page 38), or **SALMON CROQUETS** (page 93).

EGG SAUCE

2–3 tablespoons canola oil
¼ cup flour
1 cup 1% milk
½ cup stock in which salmon was poached
2 **HARD-BOILED EGGS** (page 103; discard yolks)
1 teaspoon salt
⅛ teaspoon pepper
2 tablespoons fresh parsley (chopped)
¼ cup grated Parmesan cheese

Heat oil over medium heat; add flour and stir. Quickly add milk and salmon stock and continue stirring with whisk. Add salt, pepper, cheese, and finely chopped eggs. When thickened, pour over fish, then sprinkle with parsley. Serve on chunks of **POACHED SALMON OR STEELHEAD** and with **CORN ON THE COB** (page 26) or **STEAMED RICE** (page 25) and broccoli or peas.

WARNING: Don't give raw or undercooked salmon or steelhead from western United States to your dog; it can give your dog a rickettsial disease called Salmon Poisoning Disease. If your dog ingests salmon, watch it carefully; if the dog quits eating, has a fever, and is lethargic, take it to a veterinarian quickly. Don't forget to tell the veterinarian that your dog has eaten salmon. More that 90% of dogs ill with Salmon Poisoning Disease do not recover unless given timely treatment. Humans are not affected by the disease.

BAKED SALMON

2–3 pound chunk coho or chinook salmon with skin intact
½ fresh lemon, thinly sliced
1 medium onion, thinly sliced
Aluminum foil
Non-stick spray oil

Spray 3–4-inch deep baking dish with non-stick oil. Place 2–3 pieces of lemon and 2–3 pieces of onion in baking dish. Place salmon on top of onion and lemon. Place 1–2 pieces each of lemon and onion in body cavity of fish and remainder of lemon and onion pieces on top of fish. Cover with foil. Bake at 350°F for 1½ hours. Remove lemon and onion, gently remove skin and lift cooked fish from bones. Serve with **STEAMED RICE** (page 25) and broccoli.

SALMON CROQUETS

½ pound left-over baked salmon or 2 4-ounce cans red salmon
1 egg white
2 tablespoons egg substitute (Eggbeaters®)
1 teaspoon Worchestershire® sauce
1 tablespoon lemon juice
1 tablespoon soy sauce
2–3 drops tabasco sauce
½ cup canned tomatoes (mostly pulp, not much juice)
¼ cup finely chopped onion
2 cloves garlic minced
½ teaspoon curry powder
1¼ cups bread crumbs
Nonstick spray oil

Mix salmon, moist ingredients, and spices with fork until homogeneous. Add bread crumbs and continue stirring until all crumbs are wetted. Form material into "logs" about 1 inch in diameter and about 3–3½ inches long; set on wax paper until ready to cook. Heat griddle over medium heat; spray with nonstick spray oil. Place "logs" on griddle with pancake turner. Cook about 2 minutes, turn ⅓ turn and cook about 2 minutes longer, then turn ⅓ turn further and cook another 2 minutes. This forms a triangular-shaped croquet. Cook each side another 2 minutes. Makes about 12 croquets. This recipe is almost identical with the next 1 except for the amounts and the method of cooking. Serve with **MASHED POTATOES** (page 30) and broccoli, green peas, or spinach.

LEFT-OVER SALMON LOAF

1 pound cooked salmon (poached, baked, or canned)
2 egg whites
1 teaspoon Worcestershire® sauce
2 tablespoons lemon juice
1 tablespoon soy sauce
5–6 drops tabasco sauce
1 cup canned tomatoes (drained)

½ cup mushrooms (chopped)
½ cup green pepper (chopped)
½ cup onion (chopped)
½ cup bread crumbs
1 tablespoon canola oil
½ teaspoon curry powder
Nonstick spray oil

Mix first 7 items in large bowl. Saute onion, mushrooms, and peppers in oil until onion is clear; add curry powder and stir. Add sauted vegetables and bread crumbs to salmon mixture, mix thoroughly. Spray deep 5- by 9-inch baking dish with nonstick oil. Add fish mixture and mold into loaf with rubber spatula. Bake at 350°F for 1 hour. Makes 8 servings.

Serve with **MASHED POTATOES** (page 30) and green peas or broccoli. This is a good way to use left-over **POACHED SALMON OR STEELHEAD** (page 92) or an easy meal to fix with canned salmon.

LEFT-OVER SALMON LOAF

BROILED SALMON WITH EGG SAUCE
(page 92)

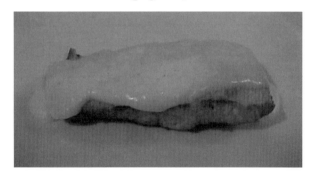

MARINADE FOR BROILING FISH

¼ cup sesame oil
½ cup soy sauce
¼ cup lemon juice
2 cloves garlic (chopped finely)

1-inch fresh ginger root (peeled and chopped finely)
¼ teaspoon monosodium glutamate
dash freshly ground pepper

Heat oil over medium heat, add garlic and ginger root. Saute briefly. Add lemon juice and soy sauce. Remove from heat. Brush liberally on salmon, steelhead, or halibut steaks 30 minutes before broiling. Also, good on thick fillets of snapper (rockfish). Just before broiling sprinkle both sides of fish with mixture of ½ tarragon and ½ cilantro finely ground in mortar and pestle.

Broil fish over charcoal (flesh side first if fillet) or under broiler in oven about 15 minutes the first side and about 5 minutes on the second. Exact time depends on distance from heat. Do not overcook fish, remove from heat as soon as fish begins to flake. For an extra delight, put **EGG SAUCE** (page 92) over the fish after removing the skin.

This is an excellent marinade for broiling chicken, too.

SCALLOPED OYSTERS

10–12 ounces medium oysters
35–40 low-salt soda crackers
1–1½ cups milk
1 tablespoon margarine
Nonstick spray oil

Spray 1½-quart Corningware baking dish with nonstick oil. Crumble ⅓- to ½-inch layer of crackers in bottom of dish. Add a layer of oysters, another layer of crackers, a second layer of oysters, and top with a layer of crackers. Dot top with margarine. Add milk until all crackers are moist. Bake at 375°F for 25–30 minutes.

I obtained this recipe from my mother. However, she made the dish with half and half instead of milk and dotted each layer with lots of butter or margarine. This was a traditional dish for Thanksgiving and Christmas dinners when I was a youngster—and 1 of my favorites. Often Thanksgiving and Christmas were the only time that fresh oysters could be obtained in the Midwest. When fresh oysters were not available, my mother used **SALSIFY** (oyster plant—page 50) to make a good substitute.

BRAISED OYSTERS

1 10-ounce jar of medium oysters
2 tablespoons lemon juice
2 tablespoons margarine

Preheat oven to 400°F. Place ½ of oysters (usually three) into each of 2 1¾-cup Corning Ware baking dishes. For each dish, sprinkle ½ of lemon juice over oysters and dot with ½ of margarine. Bake 20 minutes.

Served with multigrain toast and a steamed green vegetable, this makes a superb winter supper. Too bad that I can't get my bride to eat oysters fixed this way; otherwise, I would enjoy them much more often.

CLOCKWISE — SAUTED TOFU—page 100, **YOUNG-CHOW FRIED RICE**—page 100,
& BEEF-VEGETABLE STIRFRY—page 102

STIR-FRYS

After a time on a diet consisting heavily of blade-cut pot-roasts, potatoes, carrots, an occasional salad, and a baked apple or 2, I saved enough from my meager professor's salary to go out to dinner. The first such outing for my son and me was to a nearby Chinese restaurant. Oh, sure, these were in my younger days, so our orders leaned heavily toward deep fried foods: deep fried shrimp, fish, and chicken, egg rolls, and fried pot stickers. They were tasty, but my stomach required several antiacids tablets during the remainder of the evening. Fortunately, the chef added some dishes that contained stir-fried broccoli, carrots, snow peas, bok choy, water chestnuts, bamboo shoots, mushrooms, etc. Hey, this stuff wasn't half bad; both texture and taste were immeasurably better than the overcooked vegetables that I was served as a youngster. And, from reading, I learned that properly cooked vegetables provided vitamins and minerals, and, from experience, that they enhanced various bodily functions. I had to learn how to do this! During a visit to another Chinese restaurant with windows separating the kitchen from the dining area, I saw chefs cooking in giant round-bottomed pans. The cashier told me they were called woks. I put a wok on my wish list, and lo and behold, Santa brought me 1 the next Chistmas.

I visited the nearby Chinese restaurant sufficiently often that I became acquainted with one of the waitresses. From her I learned that sesame oil was the lubricant of choice, and that both meats and vegetables should be cooked at very high heat for relatively brief periods. They should be stirred very frequently to prevent those on the bottom from being scorched. From some of the non-deep-fried dishes that I ordered, I noted that both meat and vegetables were cut in thin, bite-sized pieces. I remember thinking "I could make a stir fry."

Initially at least, my stir-fried dishes tended to mimic those that I had ordered and enjoyed at the nearby Chinese restaurant. But, I quickly learned that recipes for stir-fried dishes, like those for vegetable soups, were flexible. If the price of broccoli or zucchini was reasonable, substitution of 1of them for exorbitantly priced out-of-season snow peas produced a reasonably satisfactory dish. And, even things that you would rarely find in a dish in a Chinese restaurant such as cauliflower also could be included in stir-frys.

I have already indicated that my blade-cut pot-roast days are over, not because of my growing culinary skill or changes in taste, but because of my physician's recommendation against a diet containing large amounts of saturated fats and cholesterol. Nevertheless, I still use a bit of beef in some stir fries. I buy top-round roasts that have relatively little fat except that attached to a sheet of facia on one side. This sheet is easily removed with a sharp filleting knife. The remainder I cut into 2–3-inch wide, ¾-inch-thick chunks that I then slice about ⅛th-inch thick across the muscle grain. The thin slices are placed into 6-ounce piles, each pile wrapped in wax paper, and the packages placed in a heavy plastic bag and frozen. Each 6-ounce package is sufficient for a stir fry that serves 2 with enough left over for 2 lunches the next day. That's hardly enough saturated fat and cholesterol in 1 person's daily diet to worry about, if intake from other sources is reasonable.

Other stir-fry dishes are listed on pages 68 & 71.

BEEF AND ZUCCHINI

6 ounces extra-lean beef
2 1-inch-diameter zucchini
½ cup fresh mushrooms
1 clove garlic
1 medium onion or 2 green onions
2 tablespoons soy sauce

1 tablespoon corn starch
1 teaspoon beef bouillon
⅛ teaspoon meat tenderizer
¾ cup cold water
3–4 tablespoons sesame oil
Nonstick spray oil

Slice beef into ⅛-inch-thick strips about 2–3 inches long; add finely chopped garlic, meat tenderizer, and soy sauce; mix well and set aside for 30 minutes; stir occasionally.

Divide zucchini in ½ crosswise, then split each ½ in ½ longways; lay each ½ cut-side down on cutting board and cut each piece into pie-shaped wedges about ⅛ inch wide and 2–3 inches long. Slice each mushroom into about 4 or 5 slices and chop onions into thumbnail-size bits.

In small sauce pan, mix **COLD** water, corn starch, and bouillon; stir. When dissolved, heat, stiring constantly until sauce thickens and bubbles. Cover and set aside.

Spray wok with nonstick oil, add ½ of sesame oil, and heat over high heat; when oil just begins to smoke add beef mixture and stir fry, stirring constantly with a pair of wooden spoons. Cook meat about 1–2 minutes; DO NOT OVER COOK! When meat no longer shows red, transfer it and any juices that remain in wok to sauce pan with sauce; mix, cover, and keep warm. Wipe wok with paper towel and spray with nonstick oil again, add remaining sesame oil, and reheat wok; add vegetables and stir fry until zucchini just becomes limp (wok should be covered for 20–30 second intervals between stirrings after initial mixing of vegetables with oil). Mix in meat and sauce and remove from heat. Serve immediately with **STEAMED RICE** (page 25) or **YUNG CHOW FRIED RICE** (page 100) and jasmine tea.

BEEF AND SNOW PEAS WITH CASHEWS

6 ounces extra-lean beef
40–50 snow peas
3–4 green onions
½ cup whole cashew nuts
2 tablespoons soy sauce
⅛ teaspoon meat tenderizer

1 tablespoon corn starch
1 teaspoon beef bouillon
¾ cup cold water
3–4 tablespoons sesame oil
Nonstick spray oil

Slice beef into ⅛-inch-thick strips about 2–3 inches long; add soy sauce and sprinkle with meat tenderizer; mix well and set aside for 30 minutes; stir occasionally.

Place cashews in small pyrex dish and microwave on high for 1 minute; remove, shake to redistribute nuts, and microwave for 1 minute; repeat as necessary until nuts are dark brown, but not black.

In small sauce pan, mix **COLD** water, corn starch, and bouillon; stir. When dissolved, commence to heat stirring constantly until sauce thickens and bubbles. Cover and set aside.

Spray wok with nonstick oil, add ½ of sesame oil, and heat over high heat; when oil just begins to smoke add beef mixture and stir fry, stirring constantly with a pair of wooden spoons. Cook meat about 1–2 minutes; DO NOT OVER COOK! When meat no longer shows red, transfer and any juices that remain in wok to sauce pan with sauce; mix, cover, and keep warm. Wipe wok with paper towel and spray with nonstick oil again, add remaining sesame oil, and reheat wok; add vegetables and stir fry until snow peas just becomes limp (wok should be covered for 20–30 second intervals between stirrings after initial mixing of vegetables with oil). Mix in meat and sauce, and remove from heat. Serve immediately, sprinkle with cashews. **YUNG CHOW FRIED RICE** (page 100) and jasmine tea are appropriate accompaniments.

STIR-FRY BEEF STROGANOFF

12 ounces extra-lean beef
7–8 large mushrooms
6 green onions
4 cups noodles
¾ cup acidopholus yogurt
1½ cups cold water
½ tablespoon beef bouillon
½ tablespoon Worchestershire® sauce

1½ tablespoons soy sauce
⅛ teaspoon freshly ground black pepper
2 tablespoons cornstarch
1 tablespoon olive oil
1–2 tablespoons sesame oil
⅛ teaspoon meattenderiser
1 teaspoon salt
Nonstick spray oil

Slice beef into ⅛-inch-thick slices about ½-inch wide by 2–3-inches long. Mix with soy sauce and meat tenderiser; return to refrigerator. Wash and chop mushrooms (¼-inch thick) and onions (½-inch lengths) including tops. Cook noodles for 16 minutes in 3–4 quarts of boiling water to which olive oil and salt were added. In sauce pan, add cornstarch, Worchestershire sauce, and bouillon to 1½-cups **COLD** water, and cook over medium high heat until thickened; set aside on warm burner. Heat wok sprayed with non-stick oil; add sesame oil and beef, and stir-fry until no red shows. Add beef and yogurt to cornstarch mixture and stir. Respray wok and add more sesame oil and stir-fry vegetables until onions begin to become limp and transparent. Turn-off heat. Add beef-yogurt-cornstarch mixture to vegetables and mix thoroughly. Drain cooked noodles and add to mixture in wok. Stir to mix well. Serve with stir-fry mixed vegetables, or steamed peas or broccoli. Serves 4.

GARLIC CHICKEN

1 whole chicken breast, skinned, boned, and cut into ¾-inch cubes
4–5 cloves garlic, peeled and chopped finely
2–3 tablespoons soy sauce
2–3 tablespoons sesame oil
Nonstick spray oil

Place chicken and garlic in mixing bowl. Press garlic chips into chicken with fork. Add soy sauce, stir, and refigerate 30 minutes to 2 hours. Spray wok with nonstick oil, add sesame oil, and heat over high heat until it just begins to smoke; add chicken-garlic-soy sauce mixture and stir fry until a large chicken chunk can be cut with wooden spoon used to stir material in wok. Serve immediately with **STEAMED RICE** (page 25) and any dish containing stir-fry vegetables.

YUNG CHOW FRIED RICE

1 cup white rice
2½ cups water
½ teaspoon salt

Bring water to boil in sauce pan. Add salt and rice. Cook over medium-low heat until water is absorbed—about 25 minutes. Cool rice and refrigerate overnight.

⅔ cup diced roast chicken
20 medium shrimp (cooked and peeled)
¼ cup diced Chinese pork
¼ cup egg substitute (Eggbeaters®)
⅔ cup chopped bean sprouts
⅔ cup finely chopped fresh mushrooms
½ cup chopped onion (green onion preferrably)

½ cup finely chopped bok choy
½ cup chopped broccoli
1 medium carrot (diced)
2–3 tablespoons sesame oil
1–2 tablespoons soy sauce
Nonstick spray oil

Scamble egg substitute in small skillet sprayed with nonstick oil. Spray wok with nonstick oil, add sesame oil and heat over high heat. When oil just begins to smoke, dump in vegetables. Stir fry vegetables until they are beginning to be limp-crisp. Add meat, eggs, rice, and soy sauce, and continue to stir fry vegetables until rice is hot through. Serve immediately, either alone or with 1 or 2 other stir fry dishes depending on how many are to be served and how many left-overs are wanted.

The Chinese restaurant that my bride and I visit most often packages left-overs for us to take home. We commonly order yung chow fried rice and a meat-vegetable dish to share; we always get a box of white rice that normally would be served to accompany the meat-vegetable dish. We freeze the boxes of white rice for use in our home-made yung chow fried rice. Actually, we like our **YUNG CHOW FRIED RICE** with rice from the restaurant better than with our home-cooked rice.

SAUTED TOFU

½ pound extra-firm tofu
1½ tablespoons soy sauce
1–2 tablespoons sesame oil
Nonstick spray oil

Slice tofu into ⅜-inch-thick slices about 1- by 2-inches; make about 10 pieces. Place in flat-bottom mixing bowl the bottom of which is covered with soy sauce. Turn pieces to cover both sides with soy sauce. Heat 10-inch skillet sprayed with nonstick oil. Add sesame oil and chunks of tofu. Saute on both sides until lightly brown. This is a low-fat source of vegetable protein. Although not a stir fry, I included this dish here because it goes well with any of the meat, vegetable or meat-vegetable stir-fry dishes.

YOUNG CHOW FRIED RICE

SAUTED TOFU

CHICKEN AND VEGETABLES

1 whole chicken breast, skinned, boned, and cut across the grain into ¼-inch-thick slices
12–20 small florets of broccoli
12–20 snow peas
12–20 medium green beans
2–3 green onions
6–8 mushrooms
1 medium carrot
1 medium green pepper

2 large stalks bok choy
½ cup bean sprouts
½ tablespoon chicken bouillon
1 tablespoon corn starch
¾ cup cold water
2–3 tablespoons soy sauce
2–3 tablespoons sesame oil
Nonstick spray oil

Place chicken slices in small mixing bowl with soy sauce and stir until all pieces are coated; refrigerate. Wash vegetables; cut onions (including tops) into ½-inch length, slice green beans (French cut—that's at a 45 degree angle), bok choy, mushrooms, and carrot; and remove stem and seeds from pepper and cut into ¼-inch wide strips. Dissolve corn starch in **COLD** water in small sauce pan; heat over medium high stirring constantly until mixture begins to thicken. Add bouillon and stir until thick and bubbly; remove from heat and cover. Stirfry chicken in half of sesame oil in wok first sprayed with nonstick oil until no pink shows when thickest chunk is cut. Dump cooked chicken in bouillon sauce. Respray wok with nonstick oil, add remaining sesame oil and stirfry vegetables covering wok for 30-second intervals between stiring. When vegetables are limp-crisp, add chicken and sauce, turn-off heat, and stir to mix completely. Serve immediately with **STEAMED RICE** (page 25) or **YUNG CHOW FRIED RICE** (page 100).

Replace the chicken with beef cut for stir fry (page 97) and the chicken bouillon with beef bouillion and you will produce a **BEEF AND VEGETABLE** stir fry.

SPRINGTIME THAI STIR-FRY

12 medium spears asparagus
6 large mushrooms
1 medium onion
½ large boneless chicken breast
Nonstick spray oil
1 tablespoon sesame oil
1 teaspoon beef bullion

2 tablespoons soy sauce
½ tablespoon corn starch
¾ cup cold water
2–3 drops tabasco sauce
1 teaspoon hoisin sauce
½ teaspoon Worcestershire sauce

Cut chicken breast lengthwise into 4 pieces, then cut each piece diagonally into 1/8-inch thick slices. Add soy sauce, stir, and refrigerate 2–3 hours. Wash asparagus, snap off ½ inch from stem end, and cut diagonally (acutely) into ¼-inch thick slices. Wash mushrooms and cut each crosswise into 4–5 slices. Peel onion and cut crosswise into ¼-inch thick slices.

In small sauce pan, add **COLD** water, tabasco, hoisin, and Worchestershire sauces to corn starch. Heat on medium-high burner and stir constantly until thickened. Cover and set aside.

Spray wok with nonstick spray oil, add half of sesame oil, and heat over high burner until nearly smoking. Add chicken and stirfry until all pieces are completely cream colored. Add chicken to sauce, cover, and set aside.

Wipe wok with paper towel, spray with nonstick spray oil again, add remaining sesame oil, and heat over high burner until nearly smoking. Add vegetables and stir constantly until all pieces are covered with oil, cover for 30 seconds, then stir vigorously again. Repeat stiring and covering for 30 seconds until vegetables are crispy tender (usually 3 or 4 repeats). Turn off heat, add chicken and sauce, and stir until thoroughly mixed. Remove from heat. Serve with **STEAMED RICE** (page 25). Serves 2 with enough leftover for lunches the following day.

Special Note: Pick medium-diameter asparagus, not the skinny little variety less than ⅜ inch in diameter and not the huge variety greater than ⅝ inch in diameter. Avoid asparagus with much white at the lower end as that part is tough and fibrous.

EGGS

Eggs are a wonderful source of protein and they are the "glue" that hold ingredients together in a wide variety of recipes. On a per volume basis, yolks of eggs contain 1 of the highest levels of cholesterol of any food in the human diet. However, egg whites have none, but have much of the protein that can serve as the "glue" in those recipes that require eggs. For those foods that require the yellow color imparted by egg yolks, use egg substitute (Eggbeaters®) or add a few drops of yellow food coloring.

In the check-out line of a grocery 1 day, the lady behind me noticed that I had a carton of eggs and several cartons of egg substitue in my basket. She asked why I had both. I responded that for breakfast I commonly prepared an omelet with egg whites and egg substitute because my spouse and I didn't care for the taste of egg substitutes by themselves. She then asked what I did with the egg yolks. In a moment of exasperation, as I don't care to visit with strangers in grocery check-out lines, I picked up a peach from my basket and responded, "After my physician warned me about the cholesterol level in eggs, I must treat the yolk of an egg exactly as I would the seed in this peach. For me, it is unedible, so I discard it." From the look on her face, I don't think that she had ever heard of cholesterol.

HARD-BOILED EGGS

Eggs
1 teaspoon salt
Cold water (an amount several times the volume of the eggs)

With sharp-pointed knife, prick a tiny hole in the shell of the large end of each egg. Place in sauce pan, cover with **COLD** water, add salt, and bring to a boil. Turn off heat and cover sauce pan. Let set for 12 minutes.

This procedure, recommended by *American Scientist*, produces hard–boiled eggs with a bright yellow yolk (no greenish coloration) that separates from the white easily. With the puncture in the shell, rarely will the shell break, but if it does, the salt will cause immediate coagulation of the egg protein, thus, little if any of the contents of the egg will leak into the water.

FRENCH TOAST FOR TWO

2 egg whites
¼ cup egg substitute (Eggbeaters®)
¼ cup 1% milk
⅛ teaspoon marjoram
⅛ teaspoon chervil
¼ teaspoon monosodium glutamate
4 1-inch-thick slices of bread
Nonstick spray oil

Spray pancake griddle with nonstick oil and heat on medium for 8–10 minutes or until oil begins to brown. With fork, mix thoroughly first 5 ingredients in a shallow pan (round cake pan). Dip bread, 1 slice at a time, into egg mixture soak for ½ minute or so. Turn bread, soak for a few moments, and transfer to griddle. Be careful not to soak bread too long or it may disintergrate during the transfer. Spread excess egg mixture on top of bread slices after transferring them to the griddle. Cook until egg mixture browns lightly, then turn and cook for an equal amount of time. Make sure that egg mixture in center of bread is cooked thoroughly so toast is not soggy in middle. Serve with maple syrup or Concord grape jelly.

I prefer commercially baked breads to home-made breads for French toast. On top of my list of breads are the multigrain or dark grain breads, or a French bread if I'm in the mood for a white bread.

OMELET

3 egg whites
½ cup egg substitute (Eggbeaters®)
¼ teaspoon marjoram
¼ teaspoon chervil
1 teaspoon monosodium glutamate
1 slice of 3% fat sandwich ham (diced finely)
1½ ounces Tillamook® cheddar cheese (grated)
Nonstick spray oil

Mix first 6 ingredients in small mixing bowl. Spray skillet with nonstick oil, and heat over medium heat until oil just begins to turn color. Add egg-ham mixture, sprinkle top with cheese, cover, and cook at medium temperature until egg-vegetable-cheese mixture is completely coagulated. Serves 2.

With the fat in the ham and ¾ ounce cheddar cheese per serving, this dish is certainly NOT cholesterol free. However, it contains much less than an omelet made with whole eggs.

OMELET, TOO

3 egg whites
½ cup egg substitute (Eggbeaters®)
¼ teaspoon marjoram
¼ teaspoon chervil
1 teaspoon monosodium glutamate
7–8 mushrooms
½ small onion or 2 small green onions
1 tablespoon canola oil
1½ ounces Tillamook® cheddar cheese (grated)
Nonstick spray oil

Mix first 5 ingredients in small mixing bowl. Wash and slice mushooms about ⅛-inch thick; chop onion finely. Heat oil in skillet, add onion and mushrooms, and saute until onion is limp and translucent. Add vegetables to ingredients in mixing bowl and stir. Wipe skillet with paper towel, spray with nonstick oil again, and heat over medium heat until oil just begins to turn color. Add egg-vegetable mixture, sprinkle top with cheese, cover, and cook at medium temperature until egg-ham-cheese mixture is completely coagulated. Serves 2.

OMELET

STIR SAUCES CONTINUOUSLY WHILE COOKING

SAUCES

A few months after my emancipation, I took 1 of my first girl friends fishing for flounder and live-bearing perch in 1 of the bays along the Pacific Coast. As she had quickly tired of blade-cut pot roasts, I decided to try to duplicate the grilled fish dish that we had eaten at a restaurant along the Coast the week before. While I prepared the fish, my girl friend rummaged through my pantry and found some stuff from which to make a **SWEET-AND-SOUR SAUCE** (see recipe below) for a topping for the grilled perch. Hey, this stuff wasn't half bad! And, it covered the spots that I had gotten a bit too brown when I was paying more attention to my girl friend than to my cooking. I quickly became an ardent sauce maker, not so much to cover my cooking errors, but to enhance the flavor of the dishes that I was learning to prepare.

SWEET-AND-SOUR SAUCE

1 cup vinegar
1 cup sugar
1 teaspoon salt
½ cup orange juice

8 ounce can crushed pineapple with juice
8 ounce can tomato sauce
2 tablespoons cornstarch
¼ cup cold water

Combine first 6 ingredients in sauce pan and bring to a boil over medium-high heat, stirring constantly with wisk. Simmer for 10 minutes. Add cornstarch dissolved in **COLD** water; continue to cook, stirring constantly, until thick and bubbly. Cool; store in loosely covered jar in refrigerator for as long as 6 months. This is excellent as a garnish for brazed, broiled, or fried chicken or fish.

TARTAR SAUCE

¾ cup **GREEN TOMATO RELISH** (page 150)
¼ cup Light Miracle Whip®

Mix ingredients well. Serve. Leftovers can be stored in a closed container in refrigerator for up to 1 week.

Good with **GRILLED SNAPPER** (page 82).

LESLIE'S COCKTAIL SAUCE

2 cups Heinz Tomato Ketchup®
¾ cup Heinz Chili Sauce®
1 tablespoon Real Lemon®
1 teaspoon grated extra hot horseradish (not horseradish sauce)

Mix all ingredients well. The amount of horseradish can be adjusted to taste. Makes a great topping for shrimp or imitation krab cocktail. Can be stored in refrigerator in a closed container almost indefinitely.

SPAGHETTI SAUCE

1½–2 cups coarsely chopped onion
1½–2 cups sliced fresh mushrooms
2 large cloves garlic
1 large green pepper
16–18 ounce can tomato sauce
1 quart canned tomatoes (Roma tomatoes, if possible)

1½ tablespoons freshly ground oregano
1 teaspoon thyme
1 teaspoon basil
¼ teaspoon freshly ground black pepper
½ tablespoon salt
2 tablespoons olive oil

In uncovered Dutch oven, saute onion and mushrooms in olive oil until onion is limp and translucent. Add remaining ingredients and cook over medium-low heat for about 45 minutes, stirring more frequently as sauce thickens. If desired, add **MEATBALLS** (page 77) last 25–30 minutes.

Blend 1 cup of dried tomatoes with 1 cup of water for a tasty substitute for the tomato sauce.

SPAGHETTI SAUCE (LARGE BATCH)

5 gallons ripe tomatoes (mostly Roma variety)
5 large onions
5 large green peppers
3 entire heads garlic
4 medium zucchini
25 large mushrooms

8–10 large sprigs parsley
2 tablespoons oregano
2 tablespoons basil
1 tablespoon thyme
1 tablespoon freshly ground black pepper
2 tablespoons salt (or salt to taste)

Wash tomatoes (but do not peel), quarter, place in pot, smash a bit with a potato masher, and cook until soft and mushy; stir occasionally. Run cooked tomatoes through food mill to remove seeds and skins. Return tomato pulp to pot and cook until reduced to ½ of volume. Start on high and stir at 2–3-minute intervals at beginning; when pulp reduced by ⅓ commence to stir constantly; and when it begins to volcano, commence to reduce heat to prevent spattering and possible burning of hands and arms while stirring. To boil down tomato pulp more efficiently place small fan at level of top of pot.

While tomato pulp is boiling down, remove seeds from peppers and cut into ½-inch squares; clean and chop onions, cut zucchini into ½-inch pie-shaped wedges; slice mushrooms; and chop parsley and garlic finely. When tomato pulp is reduced by ½ add remaining ingredients and cook for 45 minutes, stirring constantly. Allow to cool in uncovered pot for 30 minutes or so, then transfer to pint plastic containers and freeze.

To serve, thaw in microwave, add to each pint 1 small can (6 ounces) tomato paste or a paste of 1 cup dried tomatoes plus 1 cup water pulverized in blender.

If freezer is full, pour into freshly washed pint canning-jars up to within ½ inch of top, seal with canning lids and rings, and pressure at 5 pounds/square inch for 10 minutes. See section on **CANNING** in chapter on **PREPARATION AND PRESERVATION TECHNIQUES** (page 158) regarding pressure canning.

WHITE SAUCE

2 tablespoons canola oil
⅓ cup flour
1 cup milk

1 cup chicken broth
¼ cup Parmesan cheese
2 teaspoons chicken bouillon

Heat oil over medium-high, add flour, and mix thoroughly. Quickly add **COLD** milk and **COLD** broth. Cook slowly, stirring constantly with wire wisk until thick and bubbly. Add cheese and stir until dissolved.

This sauce can be poured over steamed vegetables such as asparagus, peas, lima beans, green beans, green onions, or potatoes. Several recipes included herein contain this or a similar white sauce. Use of this instead of those described with instructions for preparing the dishes will produce a satisfactory result.

CHEESEY CREAM SAUCE

¼ cup finely chopped onion
½ cup finely chopped mushrooms
1½ tablespoons canola oil
¼ cup flour
1¼ cups cold milk
½ teaspoon tarragon
½ teaspoon cilantro
¼ teaspoon monosodium glutimate (optional)
1 teaspoon chicken bouillon
⅛ teaspoon freshly ground pepper
¼ cup Parmesan cheese
1 ounce part-skim Mozzarella cheese cut into ¼-inch cubes

Saute onion and mushrooms in oil in sauce pan until onion is limp and translucent. Add flour, mix well, then add **COLD** milk, spices, and stir over medium high burner until mixture begins to thicken. Add cheeses and continue to stir until cheeses are melted and incorporated into sauce. If sauce is a bit too thick add up to ¼ cup milk a little at a time and continue to stir until proper consistency is obtained.

USES

Add 1½ cups left-over **ROAST CHICKEN** (page 58) cut into ¾-inch cubes, turn burner to low, and stir occasionally until chicken is hot through. Serve with left-over **MASHED POTATOES** (page 30) or pasta, and green vegetable. Serves 2.

Saute 2 ½-boneless chicken breasts in 1 tablespoon sesame oil in skillet sprayed with nonstick oil. Cook 1 cup noodles for 17 minutes in 3 quarts of boiling water to which 1 tablespoon olive oil has been added. Blot cooked chicken breasts with paper towel and place on bed of drained noodles. Cover chicken and noodles with cheesey cream sauce. Sprinkle with a bit of paprika. Serve with steamed broccoli or asparagus.

LESLIE'S CRANBERRY SAUCE

1 12-ounce package of cranberries
1 cup sugar
1 cup water

Put ingredients into sauce pan; bring to low boil and cook uncovered for 10 minutes stirring once in a while. Cool and refrigerate. Stored in an air-tight plastic container, it will last in the back of the refrigerator for a year or more.

Sorry, I don't care much for cranberries, but my spouse likes this dish especially at Thanksgiving and Christmas, so she makes it.

LESLIE'S CHERRY ICE-CREAM TOPPING

6 cups ground dark cherries
⅓ cup lemon juice
6 cups sugar

Cherries should be ground with the "fine" cutter blade in a grinder. Mix ingredients in a saucepan and bring to a boil stirring constantly; boil 5 minutes. Skim off foam. Fill 1-cup plastic containers to within ½ inch of top; store in freezer. It can be used straight from the freezer as this topping does not freeze firmly, or can be thawed if a looser consistency is desired. This is great on frozen yogurt or ice cream.

We can dark cherries most years. We commonly buy 30 pounds or so at a U-pick orchard as our 1 small tree rarely produces more than a few pounds—and the raccoons or robins usually get most of those. Even when picking cherries ourselves, a few with splits get in the bucket. These are the ones from which we remove the seeds and splits and grind for this topping.

RHUBARB SAUCE

16 stalks freshly cut rhubarb
1 cup white sugar
2 tablespoons water

Wash rhubarb and trim away all leaf and root material; cut into 1–1½-inch chunks. Place in small stock pot, add water, and heat over medium heat. Stir at 5–10-minute intervals until rhubarb chunks are completely disintergrated. Add sugar and mix thoroughly. Cool. Rhubarb sauce may be refrigerated about a week or may be frozen for several months.

This is an excellent topping for **SHORT CAKE** (page 119) especially when topped with nondairy whipped topping. However, it is an excellent dessert unadorned or with nondairy whipped topping. Best of all is chilled rhubarb sauce on sliced bananas topped with whipped topping. It is a great dessert on a summer day.

PLUM BUTTER

5 quarts of plums pitted, steamed, and run through a food mill

ADD to prepared plum pulp:

1 pound dark brown sugar
1 cup granulated sugar
2 tablespoons cinnamon
½ teaspoon ground cloves
½ teaspoon mace
1 teaspoon allspice
1½ teaspoons freshly ground nutmeg

Cook in pot for 1 hour or until thickened, stirring constantly. Mixture will burn easily if not well-stirred. Put in containers and freeze. Thaw in refrigerator before serving. Serve on whole-grain toast for a delightful finishing taste for breakfast.

CASHEW BRITTLE

CANDY

Ah! Candy! This is the stuff my dentist hates and my doctor advises against because of the fat some of it contains or the fat it is responsible for adding to my waistline. Nevertheless, this is the stuff that most of us crave. It has 1 redeeming attribute: it reduces the appetite for other foods. You will still crave candy, but it tends to cause you to ignore some of the other good stuff.

CASHEW BRITTLE

1½ cups raw cashew pieces
1 cup granulated sugar
½ cup white corn syrup
2 teaspoons margarine

¼ teaspoon salt
1 teaspoon baking soda
1 teaspoon vanilla extract
Nonstick spray oil

Roast cashews in 9- by 9-inch glass baking dish in microwave on highest setting for 11 minutes stirring at 1½-minute intevals. When crisp and dark brown, add 1 teaspoon margarine and stir thoroughly so that all pieces are covered; sprinkle lightly with salt.

In 1½-quart casserole, stir together sugar and syrup. Microwave on high for 4½ minutes. Add roasted nuts and stir. Microwave on high for 4½ minutes, until light brown. Add 1 teaspoon margarine and vanilla; blend well. Microwave on high for 1 minute. Add baking soda and stir gently until foamy. Quickly pour mixture on cookie sheet (pan will become hot quite rapidly, so have an oven mitt available) sprayed with nonstick oil—spread brittle very quickly with a metal utensil as it tends to harden very rapidly. Place in refrigerator and cool for 1 hour. Break into pieces. Store in tightly sealed jar in the refrigerator.

Timing is essential as undercooking or overcooking at any stage can produce a disaster. Candy is extremely prone to pick up moisture from the atmosphere and become extremely sticky.

This is cholesterol free and, in comparison with most candies, low in saturated fats. Calorie-wise, this candy isn't too bad, as the whole recipe has only about 3,500 calories. However, this candy is so good, it is difficult to stop with only a piece or 2.

My spouse is responsible for making this candy. She takes a recipe of this brittle to a local candy shop and has the pieces coated with dark chocolate. It is truly an unbelievable delight --- and highly addictive. I don't want to know how bad it is for me.

LEP COOKIES (LEPKÜCHEN)—page 117

B.J.'s FLAT-OUT OATMEAL COOKIES—page 116
Uncut on left and cut on right.

COOKIES

Cookies are tid-bits that stave off hunger, can be used for quickie desserts, or even be a breakfasts-on-the-run depending upon their ingredients and your appetitive requirements. For most people, 1 cookie rarely satisfies the latter, so a common tendency is to consume several. Unfortunately, most cookies, including several of those described herein, are a bit heavy on the fats, so some restraint in consumption is recommended. Your disregard for this admonishment is expected, especially after you try some of these recipes.

B.J.'s STAND-UP OATMEAL COOKIES

1 cup dark raisins
1 cup chopped nuts (walnuts, pecans, or filberts)
2⅓ cups old-fashioned rolled oats
1 cup flour
½ cup wheat germ
½ cup dark brown sugar
¼ cup granulated sugar
½ cup canola oil
¼ cup sorghum molasses
¼ cup cultured buttermilk or 1 tablespoon dry buttermilk and ¼ cup 1% milk
2 egg whites
¼ cup egg substitute (Eggbeaters®)
1 teaspoon baking soda
1 teaspoon cinnamon
½ teaspoon cloves
½ teaspoon nutmeg
½ teaspoon mace
½ teaspoon salt
Nonstick spray oil

Cream oil with sugar; add buttermilk, eggs, and rolled oats. Mix raisins and nuts with flour; add soda, salt, and spices. Mix wet and dry components thoroughly. Drop spoonfulls of dough on cookie sheet sprayed with nonstick oil. Bake 12 minutes at 375°F. Makes about 3 dozen.

I use a No. 30 ice-cream disher to form cookies—it produces greater uniformity and is much easier to use than spoons. For exceptionally strong-flavored cookies, use ¾ cup of English walnuts and ¼ cup black walnuts.

B.J.'s FLAT-OUT OATMEAL COOKIES

Use the same recipe except double the amount of buttermilk, increase egg whites to 3, and reduce the amount of rolled oats to 2 cups. Spread evenly on 12- by 16-inch cookie sheet sprayed with nonstick oil. Rubber spatula sprayed with nonstick oil makes spreading dough easy. Bake 20 minutes at 375°F. Cut into 5 by 6 strips to make 30 cookies. Eat a couple before they cool!

APPLESAUCE-EVERYTHING COOKIES

½ cup canola oil
1 cup dark brown sugar
1 cup applesauce
2 egg whites
1 cup flour
½ cup oat bran
1 tablespoon wheatgerm
½ teaspoon salt

1 teaspoon baking soda
½ teaspoon cinnamon
½ teaspoon nutmeg
½ teaspoon cloves
1½–2 cups old-fashioned rolled oats
¾ cup chopped nuts (walnuts, pecans, or filberts)
1 cup dark raisins
Nonstick spray oil

Cream oil and sugar in large mixing bowl; add egg whites and applesauce. In separate pan, mix dry ingredients (use 1½ cups rolled oats to start), nuts, and raisins. Add dry ingredients to wet ingredients and blend thoroughly. If dough is too thin, add as much as ½ cup rolled oats. Drop spoonfulls on cookie sheet sprayed with non-stick oil. Bake at 375°F for 18–20 minutes.

CORNMEAL COOKIES

¾ cup canola oil
1½ cups granulated sugar
5 large egg whites
1 teaspoon lemon extract
½ teaspoon vanilla
4 cups flour (sifted)
1 cup yellow cornmeal

1½ teaspoons baking powder
1 teaspoon nutmeg
½ teaspoon salt
½ cup dark raisins
¼ cup currants
Nonstick spray oil

Cream oil and sugar in mixer; add egg whites 1 at a time, beating until light and fluffy. Stir in extracts. Sift together flour, cornmeal, baking powder, nutmeg, and salt; add to creamed mixture. Chop or grind raisins and currants; add to mixture.

Spread 1 teaspoon oil on breadboard. Roll out dough ⅛-inch thick. Cut into 2½-inch diameter cookies. Remove cookies from breadboard with quick scoop with a pancake turner; transfer to cookie sheet sprayed with nonstick oil. Bake at 400°F for 10 minutes. Makes about 6 dozen cookies.

This is a flavorful, but somewhat gritty cookie. And, like the previous cookie, don't try to reduce the oil.

LEP COOKIES (LEPKÜCHEN)

1 cup canola oil
¼ cup cultured buttermilk
1 pint sorghum molasses
2 egg whites
¼ cup granulated sugar
¼ cup dark brown sugar
¾ teaspoon salt
3⅔ cups flour
¾ pound pecans
2 ounces black walnuts
6 ounces English walnuts
2 ounces dried pineapple

3 ounces dried papaya
3 ounces dried apricots
3 ounces dried dates
3 ounces dark raisins
2 tablespoons cinnamon
2 tablespoons baking soda
¾ teaspoon cloves
¾ teaspoon allspice
¾ teaspoon ginger
¾ teaspoon ground nutmeg
Nonstick spray oil

Mix dry ingredients in large mixing bowl. Chop dried fruit; separate pieces of fruit with dry ingredients. Mix dry ingredients and fruit thoroughly; add nuts. Add sorghum, oil, buttermilk, and egg whites. Mix thoroughly. Cover and refrigerate over night. Spray cookie sheets with nonstick oil. Roll out or press (with fingers) chunk of dough about ⅜-inch thick directly on cookie sheet. Bake at 350°F for 15 minutes. Remove from pan by flipping pan upside down on paper towels. Cut into 2- by 3-inch cookies with knife. Makes about 160 cookies. Cookies may be stored in air-tight plastic boxes with layers of cookies separated with wax paper. Freeze for as long as 2–3 years.

For frozen cookies that have become a bit dry, add 1 tablespoon brandy or bourbon to the container and let set in the refrigerator for a week before using.

This is a modification of a recipe obtained from my paternal grandmother more than 50 years ago. Of course, she used lard instead of oil, whole eggs instead of egg whites, and candied fruit instead of dried pineapple and papaya. This was a traditional Christmas cookie. Grandmother sometimes decorated some lep cookies with a colored sugar frosting, but I always liked the plain cookies best.

FRUITY-WALNUT COOKIES

1 teaspoon cinnamon
½ teaspoon allspice
½ teaspoon mace
½ teaspoon ground nutmeg
1 cup chopped walnuts
½ teaspoon baking soda
1 cup **STEWED DRIED FRUIT** with juice (page 146)

⅓ cup canola oil
2 egg whites
1½ cups flour
1 tablespoon buttermilk powder
⅓ cup brown sugar
Nonstick spray oil

Remove seeds from prunes. Place prunes and dried fruit in blender and blend until liquid. Add oil and egg whites and blend again. In separate bowl, mix remaining items. Add liquid and mix thoroughly with rubber spatula. Drop spoonful at a time on cookie sheet sprayed with nonstick spray oil. Bake 12 minutes at 375°F.

PIGSKIN COOKIES

⅔ cup canola oil
1 cup dark brown sugar
2 egg whites
1 teaspoon vanilla
1 tablespoons orange juice
1¾ cups flour

2 cups old-fashioned rolled oats
1 teaspoons baking soda
1 teaspoon salt
Powdered sugar
Nonstick spray oil

Cream oil and brown sugar in large mixing bowl; add egg whites, vanilla, and orange juice. Sift together flour, soda, and salt. Add dry ingredients to wet ingredients and mix thoroughly. Add rolled oats and mix. Roll out dough to ⅛-inch thickness on breadboard dusted with powdered sugar; cut with 2½-inch diameter cookie cutter. Remove cookies from board with quick scoop with pancake turner; transfer cookies to cookie sheet sprayed with nonstick oil. Bake at 325°F for 8 minutes. This cookie is a bit heavy on the fat, but reducing the oil makes them too pasty.

PUMPKIN-NUT COOKIES

½ cup canola oil
1 cup sugar
2 egg whites
¼ cup egg substitute (Eggbeaters®)
1 cup canned or frozen pumpkin
2 cups flour
4 teaspoons baking powder

1 teaspoon salt
1 tablespoon cinnamon
½ teaspoon ground nutmeg
¼ teaspoon ginger
1 cup dark raisins
1 cup chopped nuts (English walnuts, pecans, or filberts)
Nonstick spray oil

Cream oil and sugar with mixer in large mixing bowl; add egg materials and pumpkin. Sift flour, baking powder, and spices; add raisins and nuts. Add dry ingredients to wet ingredients and mix thoroughly. Drop spoonfulls of dough on cookie sheet sprayed with nonstick oil. Bake at 350°F for 15 minutes. Makes about 3 dozen.

PUMPKIN-NUT COOKIES

CAKES

In my first attempts to bake a cake, I used prepared cake mixes. By following directions explicity, I produced reasonably edible cakes. Then, I added great globs of pre-prepared icing that added more fat to an already high-fat dessert. The time came when that had to change. Also, producing a cake from scratch was a challenge that I had to attempt.

I recall as a youngster how careful my mother was in measuring ingredients, sifting the dry ones together, and mixing them with a hand-crank mixer. And, most of all, I remember how she demanded that I be still and not bounce around the kitchen while the cake was baking in the oven to avoid having it "fall." Maybe they build houses, ovens, or cake pans differently these days, but I've never had a cake "fall" while baking. Then, again, I never had a 5-year-old bouncing around my kitchen while I had a cake in the oven. That time is coming as my granddaughter will arrive for a visit early in the New Year. Also, I suspect that my mother's favorite cake—Angel Food—might be particularly prone to falling. I never baked an Angel Food cake as I never really cared for them as a youngster. They sure made pretty birthday cakes, though—all white and fluffy with candles atop.

SHORT CAKE

½ cup sugar
½ tablespoon baking powder
⅛ teaspoon salt
½ cup + ⅓ cup flour, sifted
¼ teaspoon mace
½ teaspoon vanilla extract

½ teaspoon lemon extract
2 tablespoons canola oil
1 egg white
2 tablespoons egg substitute (Eggbeaters®)
about ¼ cup 1% milk
Nonstick spray oil

Spray 8-inch diameter cake pan with nonstick oil. Mix dry ingredients. Put egg whites and egg substitute in ½-cup measure; add sufficient milk to fill measure. Add eggs, milk, and oil to dry ingredients and beat with mixer for 2 minutes. Pour batter into pan. Bake in oven at 350°F for 20 minutes or until toothpick stuck in center of cake has no batter on it when removed.

Serve with strawberries, blackberries, raspberries, **RHUBARB SAUCE** (page 110), canned peaches, or other fruit. Top fruit with non-dairy whipped topping.

This was the first made-from-scratch cake that I attempted. This cake, and all of the many succeeding **SHORT CAKES**, were outstanding successes. And, they are quick and easy, too.

For an aged friend's birthday 1 year, I baked 2 **SHORT CAKES**, sliced each in half crosswise, and alternated slices of cake, frozen blackberries, and whipped topping to form a multilayered cake. It was a big hit—and, it was good, too.

PINEAPPLE UPSIDE-DOWN CAKE

1 20-ounce can sliced pineapple   2 recipes **SHORT CAKE** (page 119)
10–12 maraschino cherries   Nonstick spray oil
¾ cup dark brown sugar

Spray 9- by 13-inch glass baking dish with nonstick oil. Arrange pineapple slices evenly on bottom of baking dish. Place maraschino cherry in center of each pineapple slice and in triangles between each slice. Spread brown sugar evenly over pineapple and cherries. Pour double recipe of **SHORT CAKE** over pineapple-brown sugar topping. Bake at 350°F for 30 minutes or until toothpick stuck in middle of cake is free of batter when removed. Remove from oven and run table knife around edge of cake to loosen. Quickly, in 1 motion, turn upside down on piece of foil twice as long as cake. If some pineapple slices stick to baking dish, leave dish upside down over cake for a few minutes; slices usually fall into place on cake. If a slice remains stuck to pan, turn pan over, remove slice with spatula or pancake turner and replace on cake.

Serve warm. When cool, cover with foil and refrigerate. Warm pieces in microwave before serving.

WHOLE-ORANGE CAKE

1 cup dark raisins   1 teaspoon baking soda
1 cup English walnuts, chopped (1/3 cup may   1 teaspoon cinnamon
   be black walnuts)   1 teaspoon cloves
1 whole orange, rind, pulp, and juice (remove seeds) 1 teaspoon allspice
½ cup canola oil   ½ teaspoon salt
½ cup granulated sugar   1 cup cultured buttermilk (or ¼ cup dried buttermilk
½ cup dark brown sugar   and 1 cup 1% milk)
2 egg whites   1 teaspoon lemon extract
2 cups flour   Nonstick spray oil
1 teaspoon baking powder

Grind first 3 ingredients together with finest blade on foodmill (grinder); run orange through last to remove last bits of raisins that tend to stick in foodmill. Cream oil, sugar, and egg whites with mixer. Add dry ingridents, then buttermilk and lemon extract. Add ground fruit and nuts last. Mix thoroughly. Bake in tube pan sprayed with nonstick oil at 350°F for 1 hour. Turn out upside down on rack to cool. To serve, warm pieces in microwave and dust with powdered sugar.

WHOLE-ORANGE CAKE

POPPY-SEED CAKE

⅔ cup sugar
½ cup safflower margarine
2 teaspoons fresh-grated lemon peel
2 egg whites
1½ cups flour

2 tablespoons poppy seeds
½ teaspoon baking soda
¼ teaspoon salt
1 cup plain yogurt
Nonstick spray oil

Preheat oven to 350°F. Spray loaf pan with oil. In large bowl mix sugar and margarine with mixer until light and fluffy. Add lemon peel and egg whites and beat until smooth. In small bowl mix flour, poppy seeds, baking soda, and salt. Add yogurt and dry ingredients alternately to sugar mixture. End with dry ingredients. Mix well. Pour in pan. Bake 40 minutes. Slice and sprinkle slices with powdered sugar.

NOTE: Cooled cake, when sliced and place in individual snack-size zip-lock bags, and kept cool, will last up to 5 days. This is a great dessert while traveling.

SPICY BREAKFAST CAKE

½ cup dark raisins
⅓ cup flour
3 tablespoons wheat germ
¾ cup old-fashioned rolled oats
3 tablespoons dark brown sugar
1½ tablespoons white sugar
2 tablespoons canola oil
1 tablespoon sorghum molasses
¼ cup cultured buttermilk
⅓ cup acidophilous yogurt

2 egg whites
2 tablespoons egg substitute (Eggbeaters®)
¼ teaspoon baking soda
⅛ teaspoon baking powder
½ teaspoon cinnamon
¼ teaspoon cloves
¼ teaspoon mace
¼ teaspoon allspice
¼ teaspoon salt
Nonstick spray oil

Preheat oven to 350°F. Spray 8- by 8-inch cake pan with nonstick oil. In bowl mix flour, wheatgerm, oats, sugars, soda, baking powder, and spices. In separate bowl mix liquid ingredients thoroughly with mixer. Add dry ingredients to liquid, mix, and pour into cake pan. Bake 28 minutes. Cool in pan for 10 minutes, then turn out on foil. When cool cover with foil.

This cake is a quick, nutritious, and tasty breakfast served with tea and orange juice. Excellent when working in the field or when traveling and overnighting in a canopied pickup.

FRESH APPLE CAKE

2 cups (tightly packed) grated apples with any juice that forms (Red Rome or Granny Smith apples are excellent)
1 cup (packed) dark brown sugar
¼ cup canola oil
2 egg whites, beaten
½ cup each dark and light raisins
½ cup English walnuts, chopped (¼ cup may be black walnuts)
1 cup flour
1 teaspoon baking soda
1 teaspoon cinnamon
½ teaspoon nutmeg
½ teaspoon mace
¼ teaspoon salt
¼ teaspoon cloves
⅛ teaspoon allspice
Nonstick spray oil
Wax paper

Spray 8- by 10-inch cake pan with nonstick oil. Cover inside of bottom with wax paper and spray wax paper with nonstick oil. Mix first 4 ingredients together thoroughly. Mix dry ingredients separately, then add to moist ingredients. Stir thoroughly and spread batter evenly in prepared cake pan. Bake at 350°F for 1 hour or until toothpick stuck in center is free of batter when removed. Turn out immediately on sheet of foil 2¼ times length of pan. Remove wax paper from bottom of cake. Wrap in foil when cooled completely. Cake can be served immediately from oven.

This cake freezes exceptionally well for long periods of time. Serving-sized pieces can be cut from frozen cakes and reheated in microwave for 1½ minutes. Serve with nondairy whipped topping or vanilla frozen yogurt.

I prepare 3 recipes at a time. This is sufficient batter for 2 9- by 13-inch cake pans—just what my oven will hold. Because this cake freezes so well, I make the supply for the entire year in the fall when my Red Rome or my Granny Smith apples are at their peak in quality. This is great when nothing else has been prepared or you are too tired to prepare anything else for dessert.

KITCHEN-SINK CAKE

1 cup dark raisins
1 cup water
¼ cup canola oil
2 egg whites
⅔ cup white sugar
⅓ cup dark brown sugar
1 teaspoon cinnamon
½ teaspoon ground nutmeg
½ teaspoon allspice
¼ teaspoon mace

¼ teaspoon ginger
¼ teaspoon cloves
½ teaspoon salt
1 teaspoon baking soda
2 tablespoons cocoa
1 tablespoon sorghum molasses
2¼ cup flour
1 cup English walnuts, chopped (⅓ cup may be ½ black walnuts)
Nonstick spray oil

Cook raisins in water; cool, add egg whites, and puree in blender. Cream oil and sugars; add to mixture in blender. Mix dry ingredients, then add walnuts, sorghum molasses, and mixture in blender. Mix well. Pour batter into 5- by 9-inch loaf pan sprayed with nonstick oil and lined with wax paper. Bake at 325°F for about 1 hour and 10 minutes. Test with toothpick after 1 hour for unbaked batter in center of cake.

I named this the "kitchen-sink cake" because it had so many ingredients—everything but the kitchen sink.

BLUEBERRY (OR GOOSEBERRY) SALLY LUNN

1 cup flour
1½ teaspoons baking powder
¼ teaspoon salt
¼ cup margarine
½ cup sugar
1 egg white

¼ cup egg substitute (Eggbeaters®)
⅜ cup milk
¾ cup blueberries
3 tablespoons brown sugar
½ teaspoon cinnamon
Nonstick spray oil

Mix together margarine, sugar, and eggs. Mix flour, baking powder, and salt. Add dry ingredients to egg mixture alternately with milk. Fold in blueberries. Turn into an 8- by 8-inch baking dish sprayed with nonstick oil. Sprinkle with brown sugar and cinnamon. Bake at 375°F for 35 minutes.

I do not recall eating blueberries before I was in the Navy where, on a few occasions, we were served blueberry muffins. I ate them, but I wasn't impressed. So, not having developed a taste for blueberries as a youngster, I developed no recipes containing them. My spouse brought this recipe to the marriage and, contrary to her claim of perpetual ignorance regarding matters related to cooking, it is she who picks blueberries, washes and freezes them, and, from time to time, bakes a **BLUEBERRY SALLY LUNN**. I'm still not enthuastic about the flavor of blueberries, but I must say this cake is much better than I remember Navy blueberry muffins. Try it; if you like blueberries, I guarantee that you will like this cake. However, if like me you don't get much from blueberries, try substituting 1 cup of gooseberries and increasing the sugar to 1 cup. It makes a tarty cake that even my spouse agrees is good.

APRICOT UPSIDE-DOWN CAKE

6 tablespoons canola oil
⅓ cup dark brown sugar
16 canned apricot halves
½ cup white sugar
2 egg whites
½ cup sorghum molasses
½ cup 1% milk

1½ cups flour
1 teaspoon baking soda
1 teaspoon cinnamon
2 tablespoons ginger
½ tablespoon mace
¼ teaspoon salt

Place 2 tablespoon margarine in 9- by 9-inch glass baking dish, melt margarine in oven as it preheats to 325°F. Sprinkle brown sugar over melted margarine in pan and distribute well-drained apricot halves over it. In small bowl, mix flour, soda, ginger, cinnamon, mace, and salt. In large bowl beat with mixer remaining ¼ cup margarine with white sugar until smooth. Add egg whites, molasses, and milk; beat. Add dry ingredients and continue beating until smooth. Pour batter over apricot halves and bake at 325°F for 1 hour or until toothpick stuck in center is free of batter when removed. Immediately invert onto serving plate or piece of aluminum foil. Serve warm.

APRICOT UPSIDE-DOWN CAKE

DRIED-FRUIT FRUIT CAKE

2 cups pitted dates cut in ¼-inch strips
2 cups dried apricots cut in ¼-inch strips
½ cup golden raisins
½ cup seedless dark raisins
½ cup dried papaya cut in ¼-inch strips
½ cup dried pineapple cut in ¼-inch cubes
1½ cups pecan halves
1½ cups large pieces English walnuts (½ cup may be black walnuts)
¾ cup flour
¾ cup sugar

½ teaspoon baking powder
4 egg whites
½ cup egg substitute (Eggbeaters®)
1 teaspoon vanilla extract
½ teaspoon mace
½ teaspoon cloves
½ teaspoon allspice
1 teaspoon cinnamon
1 tablespoon brandy or bourbon
Nonstick spray oil

Spray 5- by 9-inch loaf pan with nonstick oil, then line it with wax paper. Combine fruits and nuts, add mixed dry ingredients and stir. Separate fruit pieces. Beat egg whites and egg substitutes with vanilla, then drizzle into dry mixture. Mix thoroughly, then press batter into loaf pan with rubber spatula. Keep pressing batter into loaf pan until sufficient liquid is on surface to form a smooth surface. Bake at 325°F for 2 hours. Cool in pan for 10 minutes, then turn out on rack and cool completely. Sprinkle cooled cake with brandy or bourbon, then wrap in wax paper and foil. Refrigerate for 1 week to 2 months before cutting. Cake will keep for years in refrigerator. Sprinkle with additional spirits each time wrapping is opened. And, if it has remained in the refrigerator since last Christmas, get it out and give it a little drink about the first of November for the coming holiday season.

NOTE: This definitely is NOT your grandmother's fruit cake!

FRUITY-WALNUT CAKE

½ teaspoon baking soda
1 teaspoon cinnamon
½ teaspoon allspice
½ teaspoon mace
½ teaspoon ground nutmeg
1 cup chopped walnuts
Nonstick spray oil

⅓ cup canola oil
2 egg whites
¼ cup buttermilk
1½ cups flour
1 tablespoon buttermilk powder
⅓ cup brown sugar
1 cup **STEWED DRIED FRUIT** with juice (page 146)

Remove seeds from prunes and blend cooked dried fruit in blender until liquid; add oil and egg whites and blend again. In separate bowl, mix remaining items. Add liquid and mix thoroughly with rubber spatula. Pour batter into loaf pan sprayed with nonstick oil. Bake at 350°F for about 35 minutes. Remove from pan and cool on rack.

HALLOWEEN CAKE

Sift together:

3 cups flour
1 tablespoon baking powder
½ teaspoon baking soda
1 teaspoon salt
1 teaspoon cinnamon
1 teaspoon ginger
¼ teaspoon cloves
½ teaspoon allspice
½ teaspoon ground nutmeg
½ teaspoon mace

Mix together at slow speed in mixer:

3 egg whites
½ cup egg substitute (Eggbeaters®)
1½ cups dark brown sugar (packed)
¾ cup milk
½ cup canola oil
1 cup solid packed pumpkin
1 tablespoon sorghum molasses

Add:

½ cup chopped walnuts
1½ cups old-fashioned rolled oats

Spray pan with Nonstick sray oil

Add dry ingredients to liquid and mix at slow speed until completely blended. Pour into tube pan sprayed with nonstick oil. Bake at 350°F for about 1 hour. Cool in pan for 10 minutes; run thin-bladed knife around pan and tube; turn out on rack and allow to cool completely. Slice, sprinkle with powdered sugar, and enjoy!

ENGLISH WALNUT CAKE

½ cup canola oil
1 cup brown sugar
2 egg whites
1 cup buttermilk (or ¼ cup dry buttermilk +
    1 cup 1% milk)
1 teaspoon baking soda

½ teaspoon baking powder
½ teaspoon salt
1 teaspoon ground cardamon
1 cup chopped walnuts
2¼ cups flour
Nonstick spray oil

Cream oil and sugar, add beaten egg. Sift dry ingredients and add to batter alternately with buttermilk. Add walnuts. Bake at 350°F for 30–40 minutes in loaf pan sprayed with nonstick oil. Cool on rack.

CHEESECAKE

½ cup + 1 tablespoon sugar
1 teaspoon vanilla extract
1 cup plain yogurt
1 recipe **GRAHAM-CRACKER CRUST** (page 132)

2 egg whites
¼ cup egg substitute (Eggbeaters®)
12 ounces lite Philadelphia® cream cheese

Prepare pie crust and set in refrigerator to cool. Beat egg substitute until frothy; add ½ cup sugar, softened cream cheese, and half of vanilla. Mix well. Stir in unbeaten egg whites. Pour mixture into 8- by 8-inch glass baking dish and bake at 370°F for 20 minutes; do not brown. Remove from oven and cool for 20 minutes. Spread over prepared crust. Mix 1 tablespoon sugar, remaining vanilla, and plain yogurt—spread over pie as frosting. (Note: last 3 ingredients may be mixed with others before baking to form homogeneous pie filling.) Bake pie at 450°F for 5 minutes. Cool before serving—best to cool for 24 hours before serving.

CORN SYRUP-CHOCOLATE CAKE

1 cup flour
½ cup white sugar
¼ cup cocoa
3 tablespoons corn starch
½ teaspoon baking soda
½ teaspoon baking powder

¼ teaspoon salt
3 egg whites
¾ cup water
⅓ cup corn syrup
Nonstick spray oil

Preheat oven to 350°F. Sift flour, add other dry ingredients; mix. In separate bowl, mix egg whites, water, and corn syrup. Add dry ingredients and continue mixing with mixer for 2 minutes. Pour batter into 8- by 8-inch cake pan sprayed with nonstick oil. Bake for 30 minutes or until cake rebounds instantly from being touched lightly. Cool in pan 10 minutes, then invert onto cake plate to cool completely. Makes 9 servings. Serve with frozen yogurt, whipped topping, or aspartmine yogurt, or sprinkle with powdered sugar and serve plain.

NOTE: This is a wonderful cake for people who are lactose or milk intolerant!

YOGURT CHOCOLATE CAKE

⅔ cup flour
¼ cup unsweetened cocoa
⅔ teaspoon baking soda
⅔ teaspoon baking powder
4 large egg whites

½ cup dark bown sugar (packed)
⅔ cup plain acidophilous yogurt
1 teaspoon vanilla extract
Nonstick spray oil

Preheat oven to 350°F. Sift flour, add other dry ingredients, mix. In separate bowl, mix egg whites, yogurt, and vanilla with mixer. Add dry ingredients and mix 2 minutes. Spray 8-inch square cake pan with nonstick oil. Pour batter into pan and bake for 30 minutes or until cake recovers completely when touched lightly. Cool in pan 10 minutes, then turn out on cooling rack to cool completely. Makes 9 servings.

FROSTINGS

For most cakes, I prefer no frosting to those gooey, fat-filled prepared icings available commercially or most of those prepared from similar ingredients at home. I usually eat my cake plain or with a bit of powdered sugar or with a glob of frozen yogurt or low-fat ice cream. One frosting that I like on any of the chocolate cakes is 1 that my bride brought to the marriage. I'm not paricularly fond of coconut, but this frosting is tasty. Just don't try to delete the coconut without adding something to absorb the extra moisture. We haven't found a satisfactory substitute yet!

REDUCED-FAT COCONUT PECAN FROSTING

In a 2-quart pot mix together:

> 1 cup granulated sugar
> 1 5-ounce can evaporated milk (= ⅔ cup)
> ¼ cup margarine
> 1 egg white
> 2 tablespoons egg substitute (Eggbeaters®)

Stir over medium heat until mixture thickens. Take off heat and stir in:

> 1 cup unsweetened coconut (see NOTE)
> 1 cup chopped pecans (walnuts can be substituted)
> 1 teaspoon vanilla extract

Frosts tops of 2 cakes.

Or, can be stored in the refrigerator almost indefinitely in a plastic container with a tight lid. When needed, spoon the amount desired into a small glass dish and microwave on high for ½ minute. Spread on individual pieces of chocolate cake.

NOTE: If sweetened coconut (e.g., Baker's® coconut) is used, reduce amount of sugar to ⅔ cup.

REDUCED-FAT COCONUT PECAN FROSTING

PREPARING A GRAHAM CRACKER CRUST—page 132

Step 1.— Place mixture in glass pie pan.

Step 2.— Using knuckles, press into pan.

Step 3.— Crust ready to fill.

PIES

All my life, I had heard that making pie crusts was some kind of art mastered only by professional bakers and little old ladies. At Sunday dinner or at the annual family reunion, someone always commented on the flakiness of someone's pie crust—especially, if it were not particularly soggy or tough. I was duly intimidated. For my first attempt at pie making, I purchased a pie-crust mix that required only that water in the proper proportion be added. With the mix I produced reasonably satisfactory pie crusts, so continued to use them for several years. As I recall, I paid some astronomical sum for a box that contained enough mix for about 3 1-crust pies. In flipping through my first cookbook—the 1 that my first postdivorce girlfriend gave me—I discovered that the mix I had been buying must have consisted of nothing more than flour, salt, and shortening. All that I had to do was find the proper proportions of the 3 mysterious ingredients in the mix, add the proper proportion of water, and I could produce a pie crust equal to that produced with the mix, but at only a tiny fraction of the cost. A bit of experimentation produced a ratio of 1 cup flour, ⅓ cup shortening, ½ teaspoon salt, and 3½ tablespoons **COLD** water. This was satisfactory for a time, but then my internist checked my blood-cholesterol level and insisted that I use the least saturated vegetable fats possible for all of my cooking. So, back to the kitchen I went and with a bit more experimentation I produced a satisfactory oil crust. My recipe and instructions for the crust for a single-crust pie follow:

OIL PIE CRUST

1 cup + 1 tablespoon flour
½ teaspoon salt
¼ cup canola oil

¼ cup + 1 tablespoon ice-cold water
Wax paper

Preheat oven to 450°F. With a fork, mix flour and salt in small mixing bowl. Add oil and **ICE-COLD** water together then mix with fork in circular motion until dough forms a single ball. Sprinkle ½ handfull of cold water on a breadboard and spread evenly with hand. Lay a 14-inch-long piece of 12-inch-wide wax paper on the water and smooth it with palm of hand. Quickly place the ball of dough in the center of the wax paper and top with a second piece of wax paper of the same dimensions. With a rolling pin, roll out dough until it is nearly the size of the wax paper. Quickly remove wax paper on top and discard. Pick up sheet of dough by holding corners of wax paper and transfer to pie pan by flipping crust so wax-paper side is up. Quickly remove paper, push dough to form to pan, punch some holes in dough with fork so air and steam under crust can escape, and pinch edges of crust with tines of fork. Remove excess dough at edges with side of fork. Bake crust at 450°F for 12–13 minutes. Place excess dough on small cookie sheet and bake for nibbling.

My original recipe that contained shortening could be rolled out on a lightly floured breadboard rather than requiring use of wax paper. Also, the original dough was a bit easier to handle and tended to form to the pie pan better than the oil crust. There are some trade-offs in life. Here it is putting good health first, but still being able to eat a bit of pie over ease of handling a pie crust; surely this is a worthwhile trade-off.

Later as blood cholesterol levels continued to climb and bypass surgery became necessary, I commenced to make pies without crusts. I simply put pie filling in 4½-inch diameter individual-serving glass baking dishes (Corning H-12) and cut the baking time a bit. Well, it isn't pie, but it's better than nothing!

GENESE'S PIE CRUST

After all the effort to develop a recipe for pie crust, then modify it to reduce the saturated fat, I finally discovered the pie crust that the little old ladies at family reunions were looking for when I was a boy. When visiting in the Midwest, an old friend served a strawberry pie in the most lucious crust that I ever ate. I know that my physician would have aploplexy if he knew that I had partaken of such a delight and your's may be afflicted similarly, but I've got to pass this recipe on.

1 stick margarine (¼ pound)
1⅛ cups flour (1 cup + 2 tablespoons)
3 tablespoons powdered sugar

Mix flour and sugar, add margarine and mix with mixer until ball forms. Place ball in pie pan and press with hand until pastry is distributed evenly in pan. Squeeze pastry on pan edge between thumb and forefinger to form raised rim. Bake in 450°F oven for about 10 minutes or until lightly browned.

GRAHAM-CRACKER CRUST

My recipes for graham-cracker crusts also underwent considerable evolution. My original recipe was:

11 double graham crackers
¼ cup sugar
5 tablespoons safflower margarine

Reduce crackers to crumbs in blender or by rolling with rolling pin. Add sugar and mix. Melt margarine and drizzle over cracker-sugar mixture, stirring constantly. When margarine is thoroughly mixed with cracker crumbs, dump into center of glass pie dish. Commencing in the center, press cracker-margarine mixture into ⅛-inch layer over bottom and sides of dish. I find that pressing with the second joint of the index and middle fingers is best. Form edge of crust by pressing cracker mixture against sides of pie dish with fingers of one hand and against edge of crust with side of thumb of the other hand. Refrigerate for 2 hours before adding filling. No baking is necessary.

A 1/12th pie serving contains about 273 calories and 25 mg cholesterol just from the crust.

In an effort to reduce calories, I experimented a bit and came up with the following substitute recipe:

11 double graham crackers
¼ cup sugar
2 egg whites
1 tablespoon canola oil

Follow instructions for previous recipe, except this crust must be baked at 350°F for 10 minutes. These crusts are good for lime pies and cheese cakes, but I wouldn't recommend them for fruit or berry pies or even chocolate or pumpkins pies.

AUGUST APPLE PIE

7–8 (2 pounds) Gravenstein apples
½ cup dark raisins (optional)
½ teaspoon mace
½ teaspoon freshly ground nutmeg
½ teaspoon salt
2 tablespoons lemon juice
1 tablespoon margarine

¼ teaspoon ground cloves
⅛ teaspoon allspice
½ cup dark brown sugar
½ cup white sugar
¼ cup flour
2 teaspoons cinnamon
1½ recipes **OIL PIE CRUST** (page 131)

Peel, core, and quarter apples, then slice quarters ⅛–3/16 inches thick (1⅝ pounds prepared apples). Add lemon juice to prepared apples in large mixing bowl. In small mixing bowl, mix together raisins, flour, sugars, spices, and salt, then pour over apples and mix thoroughly. Prepare bottom crust, but do not bake. Add apple mixture and arrange so apples are packed well. Apples should be stacked 1 inch above edge of pan at its center. Dot top of pie with margarine. Roll out remaining crust in oval shape; cut into ⅜-inch-wide strips; use strips to weave lattice over top of apples. Pinch strips to edge of pie crust (a drop of water helps pieces stick together). Place pie on cookie sheet (in case the juice in the pie runs over the edge during baking) in cool oven. Bake at 400°F for 50 minutes. Let cool 10 minutes before cutting.

For September apple pie use Liberty apples, for October apple pie use Red Rome apples, and for November apple pie use Granny Smith apples. To preserve Red Rome or Granny Smith apples for pies, wipe apples with a cloth moistened with vegetable oil so that apples are covered with a light coat of oil. Kept refrigerated, apples so treated can provide apple pies of reasonably good quality through February or March. However, nothing is quite as good as the first pie of the season in August made with new-crop apples and Gravensteins are among the earliest varieties.

If you are worried about your blood-cholesterol levels, dispense with the crust and place filling in 8- by 8-inch baking dish sprayed with non-stick oil. Cover with foil and bake the same as before. This is so good that you won't miss the crust.

During a field season, a graduate student, my spouse, and I worked on several farms collecting pocket gophers for research we were conducting. On one of the farms, the farm yard adjoined the field in which we were working—and a tree absolutely filled with ripe Gravenstein apples hung over the back fence and the ground beneath it was littered with windfalls. Noting that many apples were going to waste, on the last day we trapped in the field, we backed the pickup up to the fence and, standing on the tailgate, picked enough apples for 2 apple pies. Those "stolen" apple pies were the best pies that the 3 of us ever ate.

SEEDLESS BLACKBERRY PIE

2 tablespoons lemon juice

2 tablespoons cornstarch

2 egg whites

1 tablespoon margarine

¼ teaspoon salt

1½ cups blackberry juice and pulp

¾ cup sugar

½ cup water

¼ cup flour

1 recipe **OIL PIE CRUST** (page 131)

Bake oil pie crust and cool in pan. Separate seeds from pulp of about 3 cups of large blackberries by running them through a food mill. Place blackberry juice and pulp, sugar, egg whites and salt in saucepan. In a jar, shake together cornstarch, flour, and water until mixture is smooth; add to saucepan. Heat over medium high burner stirring constantly with a wire wisk until mixture thickens. Remove from heat, add lemon juice and margarine, mix thoroughly and pour into baked pie crust and cool in refrigerator. Pie crust must be at room temperature before adding filling. Alternately, pour into serving-size containers to avoid fat in the crust Serve with a dollop of nondairy whipped topping.

If you want a real treat and live in western Oregon where Marionberries are grown, substitute this lucious berry for blackberries. These cultivated berries are a lot more expensive as blackberries are free for the picking along roadsides throughout much of the region in which Marionberries are grown.

BLACKBERRY COBBLER

5 cups blackberries

¾ cup sugar

¼ cup cornstarch

2 tablespoons flour

1 tablespoon margarine

1 recipe **OIL PIE CRUST** (page 131)

Wash and drain blackberries. Mix sugar, cornstarch, and flour. Add blackberries, stir to coat berries. Roll crust into square; line 1¾-quart Corningware baking dish with crust; allow excess crust to drape over sides of dish. Pour blackberries into crust, dot with margarine. Fold corners of crust over top of cobbler. Bake at 450°F for 10 minutes, then 35 minutes more at 350°F. Serve warm with dollop of frozen yogurt.

I can no longer eat this delicacy as the berry seeds have too much "wood" in them for my innards to cope with. I force myself to get along with the seedless blackberry pie without a crust described earlier. With an alternative as good as the pie, I can survive.

REFRIGERATOR CHOCOLATE PIE

½ cup unsweetened cocoa powder
¼ cup cornstarch
1 teaspoon vanilla
⅛ teaspoon cinnamon

2 cups 1% milk
2 egg whites
¾ cup sugar
1 recipe **OIL PIE CRUST** (page 131)

Bake oil pie crust and cool in pan. Place first 7 ingredients in saucepan and mix with wire whisk; heat over medium-high burner stirring constantly with whisk until mixture commences to boil. Continue cooking while stirring constantly until mixture thickens. Remove pan from burner and continue to stir for a couple of minutes to prevent pie filling from becoming tough. Pour into prebaked pie crust and cool in refrigerator. Pie crust must be at room temperature before adding filling. Serve with a dollop of whipped topping.

This is about as low-fat, low-cholesterol chocolate pie as is possible to make, but it is a heck of a lot tastier than one of the package gelatin-pudding mixes sometimes used as pie filling. You could use skim milk and dispense with essentially all the fat except that in the crust.

STRAWBERRY PIE

For 15 years or more, I have planted everbearing strawberries in a raised brick planter across the front of my house. Not only are everbearing varieties of strawberries much tastier than the common varieties that bear a single time (usually in June), but strawberry pies in July, August, September, and sometimes into early October are a special treat. My 36-foot row commonly produces a quart of berries a day, enough for a pie on alternate days. Recalling that while standing erect I picked strawberries that grew 3 feet off the ground makes the pie taste even better. And, somehow, strawberries in the planter are a lot prettier that the marigolds that I used to plant there.

4 tablespoons strawberry gelatin
3–4 cups whole strawberries
Nondairy whipped topping
1 recipe **OIL PIE CRUST** (page 131)

1 cup cold water
1 cup sugar
3 tablespoons cornstarch

Bake oil pie crust and cool in pan. Wash, remove tops, and drain whole berries. Place berries in pie crust. Dissolve cornstarch in water, place in pot. Add sugar and strawberry gelatin. Cook until thickened. Pour over fruit. Chill. Serve with whipped topping. Serves 8.

Once a year try this pie with **GENESE'S PIE CRUST** (page 132). You likely will salvate until strawberry season next year.

PUMPKIN PIE

2 cups canned or frozen pumpkin
⅓ cup dark brown sugar
2 egg whites
¼ cup egg substitute (Eggbeaters®)
1½ tablespoons canola oil
1 tablespoon sorghum molasses
1 teaspoon cinnamon

½ teaspoon ginger
¼ teaspoon freshly ground nutmeg
¼ teaspoon mace
⅛ teaspoon ground cloves
½ teaspoon salt
1 5-ounce can evaporated milk
1 recipe **OIL PIE CRUST** (page 131)

Line 8-inch pie pan with unbaked oil-crust pastry. Combine ingredients in order; mix at low speed. Pour into crust and bake in oven preheated to 450°F for 10 minutes. Reduce temperature to 325°F quickly (leave oven door open for a couple of minutes) and continue to bake for 50–60 minutes. Knife inserted into center of pie should be clean of pie filling when extracted.

PUMPKIN FOR PIES, COOKIES, AND CAKES

Puchase or grow a "pie" pumpkin or "sugar" pumpkin, not 1 of the giant pumpkins that sit in front of large grocery stores and are sold for jack-o-lanterns. Pie pumpkins are usually small, darkly colored, and somewhat flattened. Cut pumpkin in half and scrape out seeds with large spoon. Cut pumpkin halves into 1½–2-inch wide segments; with sharp knife remove stringy fibers. Place on rack or in colander in small stock pot and steam for 10–15 minutes or until tender. Remove, cool until pumpkin can be handled, and peel off outer rind. Run pumpkin through food mill. Store in 1- or 2-cup plastic containers in freezer. One medium pumpkin should provide sufficient pumpkin for 2 pies and 1 recipe of **HALLOWEEN CAKE** (page 126) or **PUMPKIN-NUT COOKIES** (page 118).

During a visit to Australia, I discovered that chunks of steamed pumpkin sprinkled with dark brown sugar and some freshly ground nutmeg commonly were sold in prepared-food stores catering to the tourist, working mother, and others in need of a precooked meal to take home. Served as a starchy vegetable, this is an excellment accompaniment for baked chicken. Try it sometime.

RHUBARB PIE

8–9 large stalks red rhubarb cut into 1½-inch chunks
2 tablespoons water
⅔ cup granulated sugar
¼ cup tapioca
Nondairy whipped topping
1 recipe **OIL PIE CRUST** (page 131)

Bake oil pie crust and cool in pan. In a sauce pan over medium heat, cook rhubarb and water until rhubarb is broken down completely. Stir occasionally during cooking. Remove from heat, add sugar and tapioca, and let set 30 minutes. Reheat over medium heat and cook 20 minutes stirring constantly. Pour into prebaked pie shell and chill. Serve topped with nondairy whipped topping.

GOOSEBERRY PIE

4 cups gooseberries
¾ cup sugar
¼ cup water
1 tablespoon flour
¼ teaspoon salt
½ teaspoon cinnamon

¼ teaspoon ground cloves
⅛ teaspoon freshly ground nutmeg
⅛ teaspoon mace
1 tablespoon canola oil
1½ recipes **OIL PIE CRUST** (page 131)

Prepare pie crust and set aside. Remove stems and brown flower parts from gooseberries. Combine gooseberries, ½ cup sugar, and water; cook over medium heat until berries are tender. Mix remaining sugar, flour, salt, oil, and spices into cooked berry mixture and cool. Pour into unbaked pie crust. Cover top with lattice crust. Bake at 450°F for 10 minutes; reduce temperature to 350°F and bake 25 minutes more. It is a good idea to place pie on cookie sheet in the oven, as it has a tendency to run over the edge of the crust while baking.

When I was a boy, wild gooseberries were prime when squirrel season opened in June. Wild gooseberry bushes often were abundant at edges of woodlots or in openings in the woods. When squirrels retired to their nests for the day and the hunt was over, I took off my T-shirt, tied neck and arm holes, and filled it with gooseberries. Fried young fox squirrel with gooseberry pie for dessert—I couldn't believe that anyone could ask for a better meal.

Upon telling this story to a young lady who was hired to care for our garden and springer spaniels while we were traveling, I discovered that the younger generation did not appreciate my food combinations. She declined my offer of a piece of gooseberry pie. Later, I learned that it wasn't the gooseberries, but the thought of eating a squirrel that had caused her to refuse the pie.

GOOSEBERRY PIE

PEAR PIE

¼ teaspoon allspice
¼ teaspoon ground cloves
1 tablespoon lemon juice
1 tablespoon ascorbic acid (Fruit Fresh®)
5 large ripe (but not over-ripe) pears
3½ tablespoons corn starch
1 recipe **OIL PIE CRUST** (page 131)

2 cups water
1⅛ cup sugar (1 cup + 2 tablespoons)
1 teaspoon cinnamon
1 teaspoon ginger
1 teaspoon freshly ground nutmeg
1 teaspoon mace

Bake oil pie crust and cool in pan. Mix water, sugar, and spices in large sauce pan and heat. Add pears that have been peeled, cored, and cut into 1/6$^{th's}$ lengthwise. Simmer for 15 minutes. Lift out pears with slotted spoon and place in separate bowl; continue to heat remaining liquid. Dissolve corn starch in ¼-cup **COLD** water. Add to boiling liquid and stir until thickened. Pour thin layer of liquid into baked pie crust, add pears, and pour as much of remaining liquid as needed to fill pie crust. Place pie in refrigerator until chilled (about 3 hours). Serve with dolop of low-fat nondairy whipped topping on each piece. Consume all of pie within 12 hours to maintain nonsoggy crust as pears and thickened sauce contain lots of water. This pie is so good that you shouldn't have trouble fulfilling the latter requirement.

CRUST-LESS PEACH PIE

10 ripe peaches (about 8 cups sliced peaches)
½ cup sugar
¼ cup dark brown sugar
½ teaspoon freshly ground nutmeg
1 teaspoon cinnamon

¼ teaspoon allspice
¼ teaspoon ground cloves
1 teaspoon mace
½ cup tapioca
Nonstick spray oil

Place peaches in bowl of boiling water for a few minutes, then remove skin and slice. Mix all ingredients in large mixing bowl and allow to sit for 15 minutes for tapioca to absorb moisture. Pour mixture into 7-by 12-inch baking dish sprayed with nonstick oil and bake in 350°F oven for 50 minutes. Be sure to put dish on cookie sheet while baking as juice may over flow.

Serve with lowfat ice cream.

LIME PIE

3 eggs (MUST use whole eggs)
½ cup freshly squeezed lime juice (about 3–4 limes)
1 can sweetened condensed milk (NOT evaporated milk)
¼ cup white sugar
¼ teaspoon cream of tartar
1 9-inch **GRAHAM-CRACKER CRUST** (page 132)

Prepare pie crust and set in refrigerator to cool. Separate eggs and refrigerate whites; add milk and lime juice to egg yolks; mix thoroughly and pour into prepared crust. Add cream of tartar to egg whites and beat on high speed with mixer. Add sugar slowly and continue to beat until peaks in meringue stand erect. Spread meringue on pie filling and bake at 425°F for 3–4 minutes until meringue begins to brown. Refrigerate until cold before serving. Not recommended for a low-cholesterol diet.

In the early 1950's, an uncle who visited California returned to the Midwest with a tiny lime tree. It grew and began to bear fruit. In the late 1950's, he gave me some limes from his tree. I saved the seeds from the limes and the next spring planted them in a pot. Incredibly, they came up. I saved one of the trees and by the early 1960's it began to bear. I planted a seed from one of its limes and started another tree. When moving west, the tree from my uncle's lime was given to a friend, but the 6-inch tall one had a place of honor in the back of my station wagon. Now, 35 years later, the tree, with a 5-inch diameter trunk, resides in ½ a whisky barrel on wheels and gets moved into the garage during winter. It commonly bears about 100 limes each year. Unfortunately, none goes to lime pie!

COUSIN DORIS'S PECAN PIE

3 eggs (MUST use whole eggs)
⅔ cup sugar
⅓ teaspoon salt
⅓ cup safflower margarine

1 cup dark corn syrup
1 cup pecan halves
1 recipe **OIL PIE CRUST** (page 131)

Prepare pie crust and set aside. Beat together first 5 ingredients with mixer. Add pecans and stir with spoon. Pour into pastry-lined pie tin; bake at 375°F about 40–50 minutes or until pie filling is set and crust nicely browned. Cool. May be warmed in microwave before serving. Not recommended for those on low-calorie or low-cholesterol diets. Make this pie when you are having company that will leave only 1 small piece for you!

CREAM-CHEESE CHERRY-LIME PIE

1 8-ounce package lite cream cheese
1 can fat-free sweetened condensed milk (NOT evaporated milk)
⅓ cup fresh-squeezed lime juice
1 pint home-canned Montmorency cherries (1 14½ ounce-can pie cherries in lite syrup may be substituted)
1½ tablespoons corn starch
1 9-inch **GRAHAM-CRACKER CRUST** (page 132)

Prepare and refrigerate pie crust. Mix milk and cream cheese thoroughly, add lime juice and continue to stir until mixed throughly. Spread evenly in pie crust and refrigerate. Pit cherries. In a sauce pan, mix corn starch and juice from cherries; heat over medium-high heat, stirring continuously, until thickened. Remove from heat and add pitted cherries, mix lightly, and spread evenly over lime-cheese mixture. Continue to refrigerate until both lime-cheese and cherry mixtures are set. Although not fat-free, a small piece of this pie won't raise your blood-cholesterol level too much.

CREAM-CHEESE CHERRY-LIME PIE

DESSERTS

I've always had a "sweet-tooth," so desserts were among the first items that I learned to make when I decided that my diet should include something other than blade-cut pot-roast, potatoes, carrots, and onions. Most of my desserts are listed in other categories, but some are neither pies, cakes, nor cookies so are lumped together here.

APPLE-BUTTERMILK STREUSEL

8 cups Red Rome apples (peeled, cored, and sliced)
1 cup flour
¾ cup powdered buttermilk
⅔ cup dark brown sugar, firmly packed
2 teaspoon cinnamon
½ teaspoon ginger
½ teaspoon freshly ground nutmeg
½ teaspoon mace
¼ teaspoon ground cloves
¼ teaspoon allspice
½ cup canola oil
¾ cup dark raisins
¾ cup chopped walnuts
Nonstick spray oil

Pare, quarter, and slice (3/16- to ¼-inch thick) apples. Place in 2½- to 3-quart baking dish sprayed with nonstick oil.

In a bowl stir the dry ingredients together. Mix in oil until pea size. Mix in with apples. Bake uncovered at 350°F for 40 minutes.

Allow to cool 10 minutes and serve with lowfat vanilla ice cream.

APPLE-WALNUT-RAISIN TORTE

1 cup Red Rome apples grated (keep juice)
1 teaspoon ascorbic acid (prevents fruit from darkening)
2 egg whites
½ cup dark brown sugar, packed
¼ cup granulated sugar
½ cup flour
1 teaspoon baking powder
1 teaspoon vanilla
½ teaspoon salt
½ teaspoon freshly ground nutmeg
½ teaspoon mace
½ teaspoon cinammon
⅛ teaspoon allspice
⅛ teaspoon ground cloves
½ cup chopped walnuts
⅓ cup dark raisins

Place apples (with juice) in a small bowl, sprinkle with ascorbic acid and stir. In another bowl, mix egg whites and sugars until blended. Stir in grated apples until blended. Add remaining ingredients, stir until well blended. Spread mixture evenly in pie pan. Bake in a preheated oven at 325°F for 25 minutes or until torte just pulls from side of pan.

Best served hot (in microwave reheat for ¾ minute on high) with nonfat whipped topping or vanilla frozen yogurt.

PEACH-NUT CRUMBLE

1½ quarts home-canned sliced peaches
½ cup unsifted flour
⅓ cup granulated sugar
⅓ cup dark brown sugar
¼ cup dark brown sugar
½ cup chopped walnuts
¼ teaspoon salt

½ teaspoon cinnamon
1/16 teaspoon ground cloves
¼ teaspoon mace
1 egg white, well beaten
1 tablespoon canola oil
Nonstick spray oil

Drain peaches and sprinkle with ¼ cup dark brown sugar. In another bowl mix flour, granulated and remaining dark brown sugar, walnuts, salt, spices, oil,and egg until mixture is crumbly. Place peaches in an 8- by 8-inch pan sprayed with nonstick oil. Sprinkle crumbly mixture evenly over peaches. Bake in preheated oven at 375°F for 30 minutes or until top is brown and crusty, or cook in microwave on high for 29 minutes. Serve with vanilla frozen yogurt. Serves 6.

SPECKLED SPANIEL

7 slices bread
1 large Red Rome apple
½ cup dark raisins
¼ cup canola oil
2 egg whites
¼ cup egg substitute (Eggbeaters®)
1½ cups 1% milk

1 teaspoon cinnamon
½ teaspoon freshly ground nutmeg
½ teaspoon mace
1 cup dark brown sugar
½ cup water
1 ounce Tillamook® cheddar cheese grated
Nonstick spray oil

Lightly toast bread and cut into cubes; grate apple. Spray 8- by 8-inch pyrex baking dish with nonstick spray oil; layer one-half of bread, apple, and raisins, repeat, then drizzle with canola oil. Mix egg whites, egg substitute, milk, and spices in small bowl; set aside. Mix water and sugar in sauce pan, bring to boil, and boil 5 minutes stirring constantly. Drizzle sugar mixture over layered bread cubes, then add milk and egg mixture. Top with grated cheddar cheese and bake at 350°F for 40 minutes. Cool in pan for 15 minutes. Cut into 3- by 3-inch squares. Add scoop of frozen vanilla yogurt to each serving.

Alternatives: 1. Delete cheese.

2. Add ¼ cup chopped English walnuts to each layer of bread cubes.

3. Use whole wheat or multigrain bread for ½ of bread cubes.

SNAKE EYES

2 tablespoons egg substitute (Eggbeaters®)
1 egg white
⅓ cup sugar

3 tablespoons quick cooking tapicoa
2½ cups 1% milk
1 teaspoon vanilla extract

Place egg substitute and egg white in saucepan. Beat well with a wisk to breakup the egg white completely. Add remaining ingredients and stir well. Let stand 10–30 minutes.

Stirring constantly, cook over a medium heat until the mixture comes to a boil. This will take about 18 minutes. Remove from heat and stir in the vanilla extract. Allow to sit and cool for 20 minutes. Stir well and place in single serving dishes.

Serve warm or cold. When stored in refrigerator, allow Snake Eyes to cool completely, then cover. Can be stored in the refrigerator for up to 3 days.

Alternatives: 1. Add dark raisins to mixture before beginning cooking and reduce sugar to 1/6 cup or the Snake Eyes will be incredibly sweet.

2. When Snake Eyes are removed from heat, stir-in ¼ cup semisweet chocolate chips along with vanilla extract.

A year or so after I remarried, my son came to spend the Christmas holidays with us and to visit his mother who lives across town. One evening, after dinner—and dessert—my bride ask us if we would like some tapioca pudding. My son quickly asked her "Do you know how to make Snake-eyes?" My bride laughed as she responded positively—and ever since, tapioca pudding has been called "Snake-eyes." Snake-eyes continue to be a frequent after dinner and dessert--dessert!

BANANAS AND RHUBARB SAUCE

2 slightly over-ripe bananas
1 cup **RHUBARB SAUCE** (page 110)

Peel and slice bananas crosswise—1 banana to each of 2 bowls. Add ½ cup rhubarb sauce to each bowl. Refrigerate 20–30 minutes while remainder of meal is being prepared and eaten. Serves 2.

BAKED BANANAS—page 146

Actually a microwaved mixture of banana, pineapple, orange, apricot juice, brown sugar, and spices.

FRUITS

Before I became responsible for cooking my own meals, my consumption of fruit was limited primarily to munching a Yellow Delicious apple plucked from the backyard tree or an overripe banana discovered in my lunch box while on a fishing trip. Cooked fruit was restricted to apple pies, baked apples (peeled apples filled with red-hot candies and baked until they turned red throughout—ugh!), and perhaps a peach cobbler in season. Oh, yes! My mother prepared stewed fruit that included prunes, apricots, and raisins that she occasionally served for breakfast in winter—I sort of liked that.

It wasn't long after my emancipation that I discovered that blade-cut pot-roasts with potatoes and carrots, and a piece of premixed chocolate cake for dessert, didn't satisfy my dietary needs. I had 3 beautiful fruit trees in the back yard: Yellow Delicious and Red Rome apple and Bartlett pear trees. Despite their neglect (I didn't spray for scab or worms), they still produced enormous crops of fruit each year. Most of the fruit fell on the ground to be munched on by my springer spaniels or picked up with the leaves and distributed over the garden bed to add organic material to the soil. The obvious waste became intolerable. My first step, that of controlling the diseases and pests, actually exasterbated the problem as I wound up with more fruit than before. Nevertheless, the quality of the product was enhanced dramatically.

I soon learned how to preserve some of the produce. I had a pressure canner and a book on how long to pressure different fruits and vegetables. My attempts to can Yellow Delicious apples was a disaster; I wound up with a watery, pretty tasteless, applesauce. Canned Red Romes were a little better, but not much. Canned Bartlett pears were an entirely different matter—they were superb. I knew to pick pears while they were still green and spread them on the floor under the boat to ripen so they wouldn't be gritty. And, my canning guide recommended that a syrup be added to the peeled, cored, and halved pears before they were pressured. My son and I ate canned pears and ate canned pears.

What to do with the apples? I experimented with baked apples until I got a recipe that my son and I liked (it follows). But, we could eat only so many baked apples. So, I bought a minature cider press and we ground and squeezed the juice out of buckets upon buckets full of ripe apples. With more cider than we could drink, I devised a means of preserving it. I saved ½-gallon milk cartons, washed them, sterilized them with a bleach solution, rinsed them, filled them with cider, and froze the cider. Thawed and served for breakfast in winter, it was a delight.

Then, I began to branch out, first with some strawberries, then after marrying again, apricots, peaches, plums, pie cherries, dark cherries, gooseberries, and an even greater variety of apples. The apricots, peaches, and some of the cherries didn't make it, but we now have more fruit than ever. We dry plums, apple slices, pear quarters, and cherry halves, make jars and jars of strawberry jam (my favorite) and blackberry-marionberry jam, freeze gooseberries for holiday pies (I gave up squirrel hunting, too), and pick blackberries along roadsides and other fruit at U-pick fruit farms.

Most of my recipes that include fruit are presented in other sections (for example, apple, peach, strawberry, blackberry, and gooseberry pies are in the **PIE** chapter (pages 131–140). Listed herein are some fruit recipes that don't fit appropriately in other sections.

QUICK BAKED APPLE

2¾-pound Red Rome apples
½ cup dark raisins
¼ cup dark brown sugar
1 teaspoon ground cinnamon

¼ teaspoon ground cloves
¼ teaspoon ground mace
¼ teaspoon freshly ground nutmeg
1 tablespoon canola oil

Peel and core apples. Rub each apple with ½ the oil. Place each apple in a 4½-inch diameter individual-serving glass baking dish (Corning H-12). Pack each apple with ½ the raisins, ½ the brown sugar, and ½ the spices (in that order). Place another 4½-inch glass baking dish on top of dish containing the apple; it requires a bit of juggling, but they will fit and balance. Place both units in 9- by 13-inch glass baking dish to catch excess juice in the event that dishes overflow. Microwave on high for 4 minutes, then switch apples and microwave 4 minutes more. Remove top dish and let cool a few minutes before serving.

STEWED DRIED FRUIT

12 dried prunes
24 dried apricot halves
3 slices dried pineapple
2 slices dried papaya

½ cup dark raisins
½ cup golden raisins (sultanas)
Water

Chop pineapple and papaya. Place all fruit in 2½-quart sauce pan and cover with water. Simmer for 25–30 minutes. Cool. Refrigerate. Breakfast serving consists of 2 prunes, 4 apricot halves, and an appropriate amount of other fruit. Makes 6 servings.

BAKED BANANAS

3 ripe bananas
1 8-ounce can crushed pineapple
1 cup apricot nectar
1 orange
¼ cup dark brown sugar

2 teaspoons cinnamon
½ teaspoon freshly ground nutmeg
¼ teaspoon ground cloves
½ teaspoon mace

Peel bananas, cut in ½, and slice each ½ lengthwise. Arrange pieces, cut-side up, in 8- by 8-inch baking dish. Peel orange and separate slices; cut each slice into thirds. Distribute pineapple and orange evenly over bananas and pour apricot nectar on top. Sprinkle with sugar and spices. Cover with plastic wrap and microwave on high for 4 minutes. Turn 180 degrees and microwave 4 minutes more. Serve immediately.

This is an easy, quick, tasty, and warming dessert for a winter evening. And, it is a good way to use those bananas that are becoming a bit overripe.

FRIED APPLES

2 large Red Rome apples
1 tablespoon canola oil

2 tablespoons water
4–6 tablespoons sugar

Peel (leave a few bits of skin scattered over the surface), core, and slice apples ¼-inch thick. Heat cast-iron skillet over medium to medium-high heat. Add oil, then apples, then water. Cover for 4–5 minutes. Uncover, sprinkle apples with ½ of sugar, turn them and sprinkle with remaining sugar. Continue cooking. Turn apples fequently until all of water in bottom of pan has evaporated and some of the apples begin to brown a little. Serve with **MEAT LOAF** (page 77), **ROAST CHICKEN** (page 58), pork roast, or beef roast.

FRIED APPLES

LEFT-TO-RIGHT— LESLIE'S LEMON CUCUMBER PICKLE MIX—page 149
& MOM'S PICKLED BEETS—page 150

PICKLES AND RELISHES

With a few notable exceptions, I'm not much of a pickle eater. Back in the days when my diet was beef-only, I gave my slices of dill pickles to whoever accompanied me to a fast-food restaurant for a hamburger. On hamburgers at home, I ate home-made **GREEN-TOMATO RELISH** (page 150). When we parted, my ex-wife gave me recipes for some of my favorite dishes, 1 of which was for **GREEN-TOMATO RELISH**. I made it a couple of times during my period of emancipation. Some was on hand when I courted my new bride; she loved it and added a new dimension by mixing it with light Miracle Whip® for a superb **TARTAR SAUCE** (page 107). She also brought to the marriage a recipe for a pickle mix and she talked my mother into giving her the simple recipe for beet pickles. I have appropriated both to present herein.

LESLIE'S LEMON CUCUMBER PICKLE MIX

1 gallon small lemon cucumbers
3–4 large green peppers
2–3 large onions
1 cup pickling salt (iodine free)
1 gallon cold water

24 cups sugar
12 cups vinegar
6 tablespoons pickling spices
2 small pieces and 1 large piece of cheesecloth
2 pieces of string, each 10" long

Day 1: Scrub cucumbers with vegetable brush to remove spines; remove stems, seeds, and membranes from peppers, and slice them into ½-inch wide strips; and peel and slice onions about ½-inch thick then separate the rings. Mix pickling salt and water to make a brine in a 2-gallon crock. Put vegetables into brine. Place large piece of cheese cloth over vegetables and weight with plate to ensure vegetables remain covered with brine. Cover crock with towel. Let set 24 hours.

Day 2: Drain and rinse vegetables and discard brine; rinse crock, plate, and cheese cloth. Slice cucumbers crosswise ¼-inch thick and return to crock with other vegetables. NOTE: Throw out the stem and flower ends of the cucumbers as they will become tough when pickled. In separate pan add 6 cups sugar to all 12 cups vinegar. Put ½ of spices on each of 2 squares of cheesecloth and tie with string; add to vinegar-sugar mixture. Bring mixture to boil and boil for 5 minutes. Discard spice bags. Pour boiling mixture over vegetables in crock. Place large piece of cheese cloth over vegetables and place plate on top; push down until plate is under pickling sauce. Place pint jar filled with water on top of plate to hold vegetables under pickling sauce. Make sure pint jar is sealed so it won't leak water. Cover crock with towel.

Days 3–5: Pour pickling sauce into large stock pot, add 6 cups sugar, and bring to boil. Pour hot sauce over vegetables. Replace cheese cloth, plate, jar, and towel. NOTE: Rinse cheese cloth, plate, and jar before placing over vegetables each day.

Day 6: Pour pickling sauce into large stock pot and bring to boil. Fill hot sterilized quart canning-jars with vegetables moderately loosely. Fill with hot sauce to within ½ inch of top and seal with canning lids and rings. Place on towel and cover with towel until cool. STORE IN REFRIGERATOR because pickles are not pressure sealed. Makes 4 quarts.

My mother loved pickles—almost any kind of pickles. However, we learned that she could be selective as we found, after 1 of her visits, all the green peppers had disappeared from the opened jar of this mix. We teased her about her thievery by suggesting that we would make her a jar of pickled green peppers. Regrettably, we never did, but we always sent her a quart or 2 of this mix every autumn when we made pickles.

GREEN TOMATO RELISH

4 cups ground onion
4 cups ground cabbage (1 medium head)
4 cups ground green tomatoes (about 10 mediums)
12 green peppers
6 sweet red peppers
½ cup pickling salt (iodine free)
1 tablespoon celery seed
2 tablespoons mustard seed
1½ teaspoons tumeric
4 cups apple cider vinegar
2 cups water
6 cups sugar

Grind vegetables using coarse blade in grinder. Sprinkle vegetables with salt and allow to stand overnight. Rinse and drain vegetables. Combine remaining ingredients and pour over vegetables; heat to boil and simmer 3 minutes. Place in hot sterilized pint canning-jars, seal with canning lids and rings, and pressure at 5 pounds/square inch for 10 minutes. See section on **CANNING** (page 158) in chapter on **PREPARATION AND PRESERVATION TECHNIQUES** regarding pressure canning. Makes 8 pints.

MOM'S PICKLED BEETS

4 cups water
4 cups apple cider vinegar
4 cups sugar
2 tablespoons cinnamon
2 teaspoons cloves
2 teaspoons allspice
4 quarts cooked, peeled, and sliced beets

Mix liquids, sugar, and spices, and heat to boiling. Prepare beets as indicated for canned beets (see section on **CANNING** (pages 158–159). Slice medium and large beets ¼ inch thick while still hot; leave small beets whole. Pack hot sterilized quart canning-jars loosely and fill with hot pickling sauce. Seal jars with canning lids and rings, and allow to cool. STORE IN REFRIGERATOR because pickles are not pressure sealed. Makes 3 quarts.

SAUERKRAUT

3 large heads of cabbage (about 10 pounds)
4 ounces pickling salt (iodine free)

Shred cabbage (except cores) with kraut cutter or sharp knife (no shred should be more than about ⅛th-inch thick). Place ¼ of cabbage into 2 gallon crock, add ¼ of salt and tamp with wooden masher until juice flows and no air remains in cabbage. Repeat with another ¼ of cabbage and salt until all cabbage is used and juice covers the cabbage. Cover with cheesecloth and plate. Weight plate with quart jar filled with water. Place crock in warm place (about 70°F). On alternate days, remove weight, plate, and cloth, and skim scum that forms on top of cabbage juice. Wash cloth and replace under plate and weight on alternaate days for 2–3 weeks. Odor and texture of cabbage will indicate when kraut has fermented adequately—it begins to smell like sauerkraut.

Pack kraut in hot sterilized canning-jars, fill with juice to within ½ inch of top, and seal jars with canning lids and rings. Pressure can at 5 pounds/square inch for 10 minutes. See section on **CANNING** (page 158) in chapter on **PREPARATION AND PRESERVATION TECHNIQUES** regarding pressure canning.

CLOCKWISE — steamed broccoli—page 48, **FRIED APPLES**— page 147, **MASHED POTATOES**—page 30, **& SALMON LOAF**— page 94

CLOCKWISE — cheese, **CHICKEN VEGETABLE SOUP**—page 41, **& SOURDOUGH FRENCH BREAD**—page 20

CLOCKWISE — **ROASTED CHICKEN**— page 58, **FRIED APPLES**—page 147, **& CHEESEY POTATOES**— page 29

CLOCKWISE — **GRILLED SNAPPER**— page 82, **RICE PILAF**—page 25, **&** steamed peas—page 48

MENUS

For the last 20 years of her life, my mother lived on a farm in the Midwest with 1 of my cousins. For her 90th birthday, which fell on Thanksgiving, I offered to cook dinner for her, my spouse, my spouse's aunt, my son and daughter-in-law, and my cousin and her family—24 people in all. My spouse and I flew to the Midwest to work at another university for a few days and to purchase the turkey and some of the trimmings. My spouse's aunt flew in the day before Thanksgiving with a styrofoam chest full of the remaining foods that either weren't available in the Midwest or were fresh from our autumn garden. The following is the menu followed by the grocery list; see recipes in other sections.

THANKSGIVING DINNER

Krab cocktails
Apple-roasted Turkey
1976-Bicentennial Turkey Dressing   Apple Cider Gravy
Scalloped Oysters
B. J.'s Xmas Rolls
Candied Yams   Kennebec Mashed Potatoes
Ten-minute Broccoli
Bing Cherry Gel
Assorted Condiments
Fresh-apple Cake

The adult men in my cousin's family were skeptical to the point of rudeness of my ability to prepare a meal of such proportions for such a crowd. I think that they were hoping that I would fail so that they would never be harrassed by their womenfolk. However, the following year, I received a telephone call from my mother asking if my spouse and I were coming for Thanksgiving and her birthday. When I responded positively, she asked if I were going to fix Thanksgiving dinner, too. I said, "Yes, if you want me to," to which she responded, "Everyone here would like that." The menu was essentially the same. It was the last time that I would cook for my mother.

GROCERY LIST

Note that grocery list for Thanksgiving Dinner contains home-canned items and prepared items such as **FRESH-APPLE CAKES** that normally we make and freeze. Recipes for both home-canned items and prepared items are in other sections.

1 18-pound turkey	15 small-diameter yams
½ gallon unfiltered apple cider	1 bottle canola oil
1 small bottle soy sauce	2 jars oysters
1 package corn starch	2 heads broccoli
1 head celery	1 pound dark brown sugar
1 pound mushrooms	1 dozen large eggs
1 green pepper	3 cans bing cherries
1 package egg substitue (Eggbeaters®)	2 packages cherry jello
1 box soda crackers	½ gallon 1% milk
1 package Saffola margarine®	5-pound package of flour
1 bottle white wine	1 small jar chicken bouillon
4 packages dry yeast	2 9- by 13-inch Fresh-apple Cakes
10 large Kennebec potatoes	2 large onions
1 quart Leslie's Lemon Cucumber Pickles	1 quart Pickled Beets

bread & spices for 3 recipes 1976-Bicentennial Turkey Dressing

SOME EASY AND TASTY MEALS

When I was teaching there were some extremely busy times in my life. I had little time to prepare a meal and I was too frugal to eat out as often as those busy times occurred. But, there were some rainy days that prevented gardening and other outdoor activities — the kind of days that my springer spaniels begged to sleep on their bed in the house. These days were used to prepare dishes that might last several days or could be frozen in single-serving size containers. Leftover or frozen dishes could be heated quickly in the microwave when the need arose.

BREAKFASTS

OMELET (page 104), toast (see **BREADS**, pages 1–9 & 20–21), muffins (see **MUFFINS**, pages 140–15), or **SOURDOUGH BAKING–POWDER BISCUITS** (page 21), jam, apple cider or orange juice, and tea or coffee. Sometimes I add a bit of **CREAM OF RICE** (page 23) if we are particularly hungry or have a heavy weekday ahead.

HARD-BOILED EGGS (page 103), hard cheese, slices of Chinese barbecued pork, **REFRIGERATOR OAT-BRAN MUFFINS** (page 14), apple cider or orange juice, and tea or coffee. This commonly is our breakfast while traveling or camping because everything but the tea or cooffee is prepared ahead of time.

GENESE'S MICROWAVED GRITS (page 24), toast (see **BREADS**, pages 1–9 & 20–21), jam, and tea or coffee. My bride has become accustomed to this breakfast on Wednesday mornings and is disappointed if it does not appear. Why Wednesday? You will have to ask my bride.

GERIATRIC CEREAL (page 23), **TURKEY SAUSAGE** (page 74), toast (see **BREADS**, pages 1–9 & 20–21), apple cider or orange juice, and tea or coffee.

SOURDOUGH APPLE-BUCKWHEAT PANCAKES (pages 17–18), maple syrup or honey, microwaved bacon, apple cider or orange juice, and tea or coffee. My doctor says I can have 1 slice of microwaved bacon per week, so this is Saturday-morning's breakfast. Why Saturday? Because I have more time to make all this stuff.

SOURDOUGH WAFFLES (page 18), maple syrup or honey, margarine, microwaved bacon, apple cider or orange juice, and tea or coffee.

FRENCH TOAST FOR TWO (page 104), microwaved bacon, maple syrup or honey, margarine, apple cider or orange juice, and tea or coffee.

DINNERS

PRESSURE-COOKER STEW (page 79), **SOURDOUGH BAKING POWDER BISCUITS** (page 21), and Strawberry Jam. Although this meal is quick and easy, it requires some coordination to get everything ready at the same time. So, you can't watch the evening news or engage in extracuricular activities while preparing this meal. This can be prepared in about 30 minutes including preparation of vegetables.

SAUTED TURKEY STEAK (page 72), **CHEESEY CREAM SAUCE** (page 109), **MASHED POTATOES** (page 30, and steamed carrots. This takes a bit of juggling, because the Cream Sauce has to be stirred constantly and it is necessary to saute the Turkey Steak at the same time. Or, you can cook the sauce then the turkey, but the sauce is better when it is freshly cooked and very hot. This can be prepared in about 25 minutes

SPLIT CHICKEN (page 59), **FALAFIL CAKES** (page 33), and steamed broccoli. Preparation of this meal takes longer (about 75 minutes) than some of the others, but you get a couple of breaks to watch the evening news or read the paper. Or, after starting the chicken, you could water the garden, pick a head of broccoli, and feed the dogs before cooking the broccoli and **FALAFIL CAKES** 10 minutes before the chicken is ready.

Broiled salmon or steelhead (see **MARINADE FOR BROILING FISH**–page 94), **EGG SAUCE** (page 92), **CORN ON THE COB** (page 26), steamed broccoli and steamed cauliflower. This is a quick and easy meal that is really sumptious. It is what my bride calls an "Oinker Meal" because it is really "high on the hog." The fish may be a bit expensive, but if you are trying to impress someone, it will be well worth it. This can be prepared in about 25–30 minutes.

BROILED CHICKEN (page 60), **STEAMED RICE** (page 25), and steamed English peas. This meal requires little thought if you are using frozen chicken and frozen peas other than remembering to thaw the chicken and soaking it in the marinade for a couple of hours before it is time to cook. Turn on the stove to heat water for the rice just before putting the chicken on the broiling pan and sprinkling it with herbs. Then your meal will be ready to eat in about 24–25 minutes after putting the chicken under the broiler.

STIR-FRY BEEF STROGANOFF (page 99) and steamed broccoil. If beef is prepared earlier and frozen in 6-ounce packages, then the most time required is to thaw the beef (only a couple of hours or so in cold water). Otherwise, preparation time is only about 20–25 minutes for this really "stick-to-the-ribs" meal.

STIR-FRY CHICKEN AND VEGETABLES (page 102), **YUNG CHOW FRIED RICE** (page 100), and **SAUTED TOFU** (page 101). This meal requires considerable prep-time to wash and chop the vegetables, and to slice the tofu, but only about 10 minutes to cook. You will need 2 woks, a 10-inch skillet, and a small sauce pan. And, when it comes time to cook and serve, an extra set of hands is mighty useful. A pot of jasmine tea makes this a super meal.

Spaghetti with **SPAGHETTI SAUCE** (page 108) and **MEATBALLS** (page 77) with a chunk of **SOURDOUGH FRENCH BREAD** (page 20) and frozen yogurt for dessert. This can be prepared in about 20–25 minutes with frozen meatballs and bread that you baked last Saturday.

KRAB MOSTACCIOLI (page 32) and **FRESH APPLE CAKE** (page 122). By hurrying—and efficient use of the stove to cook pasta and the microwave to thaw crab and cake, this meal can be prepared in about 20–25 minutes. With a stock pot, wok, cutting board, microwaveable dish, and mixing bowls in addition to plates, cutlery, and glasses to wash or put in the dishwasher, cleanup time may be extended a bit.

BLADE-CUT POT ROAST, POTATOES, CARROTS, and **ONIONS** (described on top of page xi). After having lived on a diet consisting largely of this for so long, I could hardly fail to include it among the easy meals. It does take a bit of time to cook, but from experience, I can attest that it can be overdone. Not recommended for the only evening meal in the diet. This can be prepared in about 1½ hours. You have time to watch the evening news, work a bit in the garden, walk the dogs, or prepare a wonderful dessert.

GOBBLER LASAGNA (page 31), canned green beans, and **FRESH APPLE CAKE** (page 122). From frozen lasagna and cake, this can be prepared in about 15 minutes.

UNSTUFFED PEPPERS (page 75), **MASHED POTATOES** (page 30), AND **RHUBARB SAUCE** (page 110) on **SHORT CAKE** (page 119). The cake can be baked ahead and refrigerated for a week or so. From frozen unstuffed peppers and rhubarb sauce, this can be prepared in about 20 minutes.

Turkey kielbasa, **SAUERKRAUT** (page 151), and steamed carrots, potatoes, and small onions. Scrub carrots and cut into ¾-inch lengths. Peel potatoes and cut into 1-inch cubes. Peel onions, leave whole. Place carrots, potatoes, and onions (in that order) on steamer rack over ¾ inch of water in large (2½ quart) sauce pan. Bring to a boil and steam for 20 minutes or until potatoes and carrots can be pierced easily with fork. Place 2-inch lengths of kielbasa on top of sauerkraut in separate sauce pan. Cover sauce pan and place on medium burner and allow to heat while other vegetables cook. Stir occasionally. Serve with mustard. Serves 4.

PRESERVING FRUITS AND VEGETABLES

As my garden beds increased in number and increased in productivity because of double cropping, I began to produce far more food than I could eat or give to my friends. Students in my autumn-term course threatened to complain to the dean if I came to class with another grocery bag full of zucchinis. Unfortunately, production was seasonal so I had too much in summer and autumn, and little or none in winter and early spring. I had to learn how to preserve some of my produce. I had a pressure canner and a supply of canning jars, and I had a freezer. Also, I knew that I could not experiment as I had done with blade-cut pot-roasts and other dishes that I tried when I became the cook because improperly preserved foods can be deadly. I bought a book! Initially, I followed the directions explicity, but I soon learned that the amount of sugar or salt was not to my liking, or I liked some vegetables cut into chunks rather than sliced, or I liked different spices than the recipes called for. So, like so much of cooking, some things could be changed a bit to suit my tastes. However, everything that I read on the subject warned against reducing preserving times, temperatures, or canner pressures. That's logical. Organisms in items to be preserved must either be destroyed or prevented from growing to avoid decomposition of the foods or production of toxins therein. Also, I soon learned that I liked some fruits and vegetables better frozen than canned and vice versa. My recipes are for how I believe specific fruits are best preserved.

PREPRATION AND PRESERVATION TECHNIQUES

Food may be preserved by cooking, freezing, or drying. All these techniques have in common the prevention of growth of microorganisms: cooking by killing them, freezing and drying by preventing their growth and reproduction. Cooking may be accomplished by pressure canning or by a boiling-water bath. I use a pressure cooker exclusively because I am certain that microorganisms and their spores are destroyed by the higher temperature than the 212°F that can be obtained with boiling water. However, boiling-water bath is satisfactory for acid foods such as tomatoes.

CANNING

My pressure canner holds 7 quart or 9 pint canning jars, so all my recipes are in units of of those amounts. Wash jars and rinse with hot water before filling. Fill jars with material to be preserved, but leave about ¾-inch of air-space at the top. Be sure to wipe lip of jar with a clean cloth before attaching the lid. Filled jars should be placed in canner with water about ½–¾ the height of the jars. With the canner on a large stove element turned to the highest setting, the lid should be closed and the vent on top opened. Allow steam to vent for 10 minutes. Close vent and allow pressure inside of the canner to rise to the designated level before adjusting heat to hold the proper pressure. Cooking time should timed from when pressure attains designated level. Often it is necessary to partially remove pressure cooker from burner for a short time so pressure will not exceed designated level. At end of designated time, remove canner from burner and set on metal rack. A small fan can be turned on canner to cause pressure (and temperature) to fall more rapidly. When guage indicates pressure has dropped to zero, open vent; if no steam escapes from opened vent it is safe to remove lid from canner. Open lid by tilting it so face and hands are protected from steam remaining in canner. Cover opened canner with a towel for 2–5 minutes before removing jars. Remove jars, place on towel, and cover with towel until cool; cooling may require several hours. When cool, wash jars and store in cartons to protect fruit and vegetables from the light.

WARNING: While pressure canner is in use, watch pressure guage continuously. Don't go to the garden for additional vegetables. Don't call someone on the telephone and don't talk to anyone unless the telephone can be brought to where the canner is located. And, don't be distracted by preparing fruits or vegetables for the "next load." WATCH THE PRESSURE GUAGE!

When I was a teenager, our next-door neighbor who was somewhat of a gossip was canning green beans 1 morning when her telephone rang. The pressure in her cooker was rising when she answered the telephone. While she was distracted by neighborhood goings-on, the pressure increased to the point that it blew the lid off of her cooker through the floor into the bedroom above. The lid was followed by a stream of super-heated water and green beans. Not only was a complete remodeling of the kitchen necessary, but the bedroom required extensive repair also. WATCH THE PRESSURE GUAGE!

The following is a list of canner pressures and cooking times for the more common fruits and vegetables:

Food Item	Pressure (lbs/in^2)	Time (minutes)
Fruits (pints or quarts)		
Apricots	5	10
Blackberries	5	8
Cherries	5	10
Peaches	5	10
Pears	5	10
Plums	5	10
Rhubarb	5	5
Vegetables (as indicated)		
Beets (pints)	10	25
Corn (pints)	10	55
Green beans (pints)	10	25
Peas (pints)	10	40
Sauerkraut (pints)	5	10
Spaghetti sauce (quarts)	10	15
Tomatoes (quarts)	5	10
Tomato juice (quarts)	5	10
Green tomato relish (pints)	5	10

FRUITS

Apricots—Cut apricots in half and remove seeds and stem bases. Mix 4 cups sugar with 12 cups water in large stock pot; stir to dissolve sugar and heat to a low boil. Add apricot halves to syrup and simmer until most of them begin to soften and can be flattened by the touch of a wooden spoon. Remove from heat, pack freshly cleaned canning-jars with fruit, add 1 teaspoon ascorbic acid powder and syrup to ¾ inch of top of jar. Slide knife alongside apricots to remove air. Wipe rim of jar with clean towel. Seal jars with canning lids and rings. Pressure can as indicated above. I prefer Moorpark apricots as they do not fragment when canned. NOTE: Excess syrup can be sealed in jars and either pressure canned or refrigerated and used in canning peaches. In fact, I prefer peaches canned with syrup used in processing apricots.

Cherries—Wash cherries; set aside those with splits or other irregularities. Heat syrup of 3 cups sugar and 4 cups of water for each 7 quarts of cherries to be canned; stir to dissolve sugar. Pack cherries in freshly cleaned canning-jars, fill with syrup to ¾ inch of top, Wipe rim of jar with clean towel, and seal jars with canning lids and rings. Pressure can as indicated above.

Peaches—Place 8 or 10 peaches in large mixing bowl and cover with boiling water until skins begin to slip. Pour off hot water, peel peaches, remove seeds, and slice peaches ½–inch thick. Repeat process, storing slices in large mixing bowl or plastic bucket, until enough for 7 quarts has accumulated. Pack slices in freshly cleaned canning-jars, add syrup left over from canning apricots or prepare a syrup of 1 cup sugar per 3 cups water, add 1 teaspoon ascorbic acid powder per jar. Don't forget to leave ¾-inch of air space. Slide knife alongside peaches to remove air. Wipe rim of jar with clean towel. Seal jars with lids and rings and pressure can as indicated above. I prefer Veteran peaches because of their flavor and texture when canned. About 15 pounds of peaches is sufficient for 7 quarts.

Pears—To avoid pears with a gritty texture, pick full-grown fruit while still green and hard. To ripen, spread pears on plastic in an area protected from springer spaniels and other possible hazards; I spread pears on a plastic sheet under the boat trailer in the garage. When pears turn yellow, but have not yet softened, they are ready to can. Wash pears and peel with potato peeler. Place peeled pears in clean bucket with about ¼ cup vinegar per gallon of water. When bucket is full of submerged pears, remove one at a time, split in half and remove stem and core. Split halves to form quarters and pack quarters into freshly cleaned canning-jars. Add 1 teaspoon ascorbic acid powder to each jar and fill jars to ¾ inch of top with hot syrup consisting of 1 cup of sugar per 4 cups of water (4½ cups sugar and 18 cups water is sufficient syrup for 21 quarts of pears). Slide knife alongside pears to remove air bubbles, wipe rim of jar with clean towel, and seal with canning lid and rings. Pressure can as indicated above.

VEGETABLES

The preparation and preservation processes described herein will produce tasty and safe canned vegetables. Nevertheless, if from some error, the preservation process is incomplete, it is possible for the organism that produces the toxin responsible for botulism poisoning to grow in sealed jars without air. This is a particularly deadly toxin, thus it is prudent to be cautious. So to be on the safe side upon opening jars of home-canned vegetables (except tomatoes), never eat any without first heating them to boiling. The high temperature destroys the toxin. Tomatoes (and tomato juice) are an exception because the organism cannot grow in this highly acid vegetable.

Beets—Cut tops from beets leaving at least 2 inches of stems. Wash beets and place in large stock pot (a stock pot with removable colander is preferred). Cover beets with water, add cover to stock pot, and heat to boiling. Reduce heat to low boil and continue cooking until beets can be penetrated with fork easily. Remove beets from pot and spray with cold water until beets can be handled. Tops, skins, and roots should slip from beets easily. Leave small beets whole, but cut larger beets into wedges about ¾-inch thick. Pack into freshly cleaned pint canning-jars, add ½ teaspoon salt, fill with boiling water to within ¾ inch of top, wipe rim of jar with clean towel, and seal with canning lids and rings. Pressure can as indicated above.

Green beans—Pick beans when seeds are small as seeds in more mature beans are pasty. Wash freshly picked beans and remove stems. Cut beans into 1½-inch lengths. Bring water sufficient to cover 1 gallon of cut beans to boiling in large stock pot. Add beans and bring to boil, reduce heat to low boil, and cook beans for 5 minutes. Remove beans with slotted spoon and fill washed and sterilized (fill with boiling water) jars with beans; shake jars and tamp gently to pack beans into freshly cleaned canning-jars. Add ½ teaspoon salt per pint jar. Add hot water in which beans were cooked to ¾ inch of top of jars. Wipe rim of jar with clean towel. Seal jars with canning lids and rings, and pressure can as indicated above.

Tomatoes—Place 8–10 ripe tomatoes in large mixing bowl and cover with boiling water. When skins begin to split, remove tomatoes, slip skins from tomatoes, and remove cores. Pack tomatoes into freashly washed canning-jars to with ¾ inch of top, add 1 teaspoon salt per quart jar, wipe rim of jar with clean towel, and seal jars with canning lids and rings. Pressure can as indicated above.

FREEZING

Freezing most produce is much simpler and requires less effort and time than canning, and in many instances produces much more flavorful foods. However, some produce does not freeze well, and in other instances, it is more convenient and economical to use canned foods when only part of the container is needed for a meal as left overs can be refrigerated, whereas some left-over frozen foods deteriorate rapidly even under refrigeration. For example, for several years I froze peaches, but soon after thawing they begin to deteriorate rapidly, so it was "eat the whole package, or throw away what I didn't eat." I shifted to canning peaches then, when I use part of a jar, I refrigerate the uneaten portion for a few days until I want more peaches. No waste and no deterioration of the left-over fruit. However, opened jars of fruit left in the refrigerator too long will mold and become unetable.

FRUITS

Berries—For blackberries, marionberries, blueberries, and raspberries, simply wash freshly picked fruit, discard under-ripe and over-ripe fruit, and spread evenly 1-layer thick on large cookie sheets. Place in freezer until completely frozen. Quickly package appropriate lots in plastic bags and store in freezer. Be sure to remove as much air as possible from plastic bags. Gooseberries can be prepared and preserved similarly after removing stems and dried flowers.

VEGETABLES

Before being frozen, beans, peas, spinach, and some other vegetables must be steamed for a few minutes to destroy certain enzymes in them to maintain quality. After steaming, it is imperative to chill the vegetables as quickly as possible to stop the cooking process. I half fill a sink with cold water and add chunks of ice then repeatedly submerge colander containing steamed vegetables to cool them quickly before packaging. Packaged vegetables are placed in the freezer compartment of the kitchen refrigerator immediately, then moved to the freezer at the end of the preserving session.

Peas—Pick fully formed peas before they become starchy. Hull peas, separating out any over-mature ones. Wash peas, pick out foreign material, and drain. Heat ½-inch water to boiling in stock pot into which small colandar will fit. Place 1 cup peas in colandar and steam for 3 minutes. Remove colander, chill peas in ice water, package in plastic bags, and place in freezer. Remove as much air as possible from plastic bags. Each bag will make 2 servings. Freeze over-mature peas in separate ½-cup packages for use in vegetable soup.

Lima beans—Follow instructions for peas. Package over-mature limas in ½-cup lots for vegetable soup.

Mature green beans—Select mature beans just before they begin to dry as they hull easily. Follow instructions for peas. Package hulled beans in ½-cup lots for vegetable soup.

Spinach—Pick large crinkled leaves while they are still crisp and tender. Wash thoroughly, remove any foreign material, and drain. Steam for 3 minutes, chill quickly in ice water, squeeze out as much water as possible, package in plastic bags, and place in freezer.

Corn—AS EARS FOR CORN ON THE COB: Pick ears; remove husks, silks, and tips from freshly picked ears; package in plastic bags, and place in freezer as quickly as possible. DO NOT WASH. Ears will last 6–8 months in good condition if the entire process is handled expeditiously.

AS GRAIN REMOVED FROM COBS: Pick ears, remove husks, silks, and tips from freshly picked ears. Place ears in boiling water in large stock pot, bring water back to a boil, and cook ears for 10 minutes. Cool ears as quickly as possible in ice-water bath. When ears are cool enough to handle, remove grain from cobs. I use a special device designed to remove grains from entire ear in one pass (see picture). Package 1-cup measures of grains in plastic bags. Flatten bags to remove air and freeze quickly as possible. The thin sheets of corn may be broken easily if less than a cup is needed.

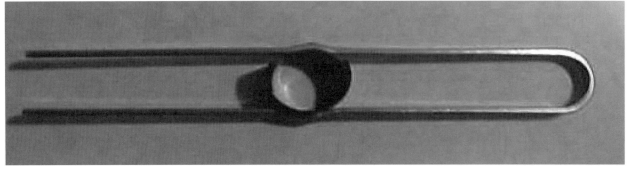

DEVICE FOR REMOVING CORN FROM COB

In preserving as ears or grains removed from cobs, delay in processing ears after picking will result in sugars being converted to starches thereby reducing quality of corn. Handle the process from field to freezer as quickly as possible.

Green peppers—Wash peppers, remove tops, seeds, and membranes. Cut peppers into half or thirds. Place in plastic bags and freeze. Frozen peppers, cut into small pieces, are good in vegetable soups, pilafs, and spaghetti sauces.

Tomatoes—Place 8–10 fully ripe tomatoes in large mixing bowl and cover with boiling water. When skin begins to slip, remove from water, cool in cold-water bath, peel, core, place in plastic bags, and freeze. Frozen tomatoes are good in soups.

DRYING

The drying process not only compacts fruits and vegetables it also concentrates flavors. Thus, fruits like apples, cherries, peaches, pears, plums, and tomatoes make wonderful snacks when dried. Dried tomatoes also are good when added to spagetti sauce, lasgana, and soups. And vegetables like corn when dried add a wonderful flavor to soups quite different from frozen corn. Dried fruits also are a good source of fiber and make welcomed gifts.

Do remember that drying will continue as the produce cools to room temperature. So, do not keep fruits in dehydrator until they are completely dry or chips will be produced. If this does happen, do not despair. Just leave the storage container open for a day or so and the chips will pick up moisture from the air and soften a bit.

Store dried fruits and vegetables in zip-lock plastic bags or jars in pantry or a kitchen cabinet. If dried properly, the dried produce will remain in good condition for a year or longer if you can keep from eating it all sooner.

Careful selection of individual fruits and vegetables is the key to successful drying. All produce should be free of blemishes and bruises and fully ripe but not soft. Fruits, such as cherries, peaches, and pears, should have a high sugar content. For example, pears should be more ripe than desired for canning but not soft and tomatoes should be ripe enough that they have a strong fragrance. Corn should be processed and placed in the dehydrator as soon as possible after picking. Many books suggest pretreating fruits and vegetables with either ascorbic acid or a salt-water solution before drying to preserve color and quality of the dried products. However, I have found that if fruits and vegetables are in good condition and dried properly that pretreatment is not necessary to maintain color and quality of the final product.

Apples—Wash, peel, core, and cut ⅛-inch slices crosswise. Place on dehydrator trays in 1 layer and dry for approximately 8 hours. Slices should feel tough, but not hard when still hot from the dehydrator.

Cherries—Wash, cut in half, and remove pit. Place on dehydrator trays with cut side up in 1 layer and dry for approximately 8 hours. Halves should feel tough, but not hard when still hot from the dehydrator.

Corn—Prepare as for frozen corn kernals removed from the cob. Spread out 1-layer thick and dry until hard. The drying process should take about 12 hours.

Peaches—Wash, peel, cut in wedges, and remove pit. Place on dehydrator trays in 1 layer and dry for approximately 8 hours. Wedges should feel tough, but not hard when still hot from the dehydrator.

Pears—Wash, peel, cut in quarters lengthwise, and core. Place on dehydrator trays in 1 layer and dry for approximately 30–36 hours. The drying time is so long because pears contain so much water. I call dried pear quarters "pear candy." Needless to say, they are quite a hit with children.

Plums—Wash, cut in half, and remove pit. Place on dehydrator trays with cut side up in 1 layer and dry for approximately 12–14 hours. Halves should feel tough, but not be hard when still hot from the dehydrator.

Tomatoes—Wash, DO NOT peel, and slice ¼-inch thick. Discard slices including the stem and flower ends. Place on dehydrator trays in 1 layer and dry for approximately 16–18 hours. Slices should feel tough, but not be hard when still hot from the dehydrator.

STORING

Some vegetables can be stored without being canned or frozen, but require some special conditions and sometimes a bit of preparation.

Potatoes—Before digging potatoes, do not irrigate for several days so soil can dry. Dig potatoes, spread on plastic in shaded area, and place oscillating electric fan at 1 side of plastic. Allow potatoes to dry out of direct sunlight under fan for 24 hours. Store potatoes in wooden bushel baskets in a cool place in ABSOLUTE DARKNESS. I place 2 baskets with potatoes on 2 2 by 4's in the coolest corner of my garage and cover top, sides, and bottoms of baskets with 3 layers of black plastic. Potatoes allowed to remain in lighted areas will turn green and become toxic. Don't refrigerate potatoes as some of the starches will convert to sugars.

Onions—Pull mature onions and allow them to remain on the surface until tops dry completely. Remove dried tops and store in wooden bushel baskets in a cool place. Cover bushel baskets with old towel. Check onions at about weekly intervals to ascertain if they were too wet when placed in baskets. Sometimes it is necessary to dry onions under a fan as described for potatoes.

Apples—Pick blemish-free apples and handle carefully—do not bruise. Wipe apples with cloth saturated with canola oil. Place apples in bucket in refrigerator. Some varieties can be stored successfully for several months. Red Rome and Granny Smith apples will store well; Yellow Delicious do not store well for long.

Canned fruits and vegetables—Place jars in boxes with cardboard separaters between jars. Close boxes to avoid light on jars. Store boxes in cool place, but do not permit materials to freeze.

TRICKS

Despite all the admonishments in recipes and on packages of prepared foods, I was forever making mistakes. Usually, I was in too great of a hurry to read and remember whether this item was added first or last, whether something had to be cooled first, or whether or not to put a lid on a jar. While an undergraduate student, I failed to recognize that yeast dough placed in a tightly sealed jar could explode. The result was a heck of a mess and an irrate roommate and a landlady who was nearly scared out of her wits. I returned to our appartment to find my landlady at the open door to our apartment and my roommate standing on the kitchen table covered with shards of dough-covered glass while he scraped a glob of dough off the ceiling and turned the air blue by reciting his newly derived names for me and my culinary skills. He banished me from the kitchen for the remainder of the semester, another reason for my failure to learn to cook while young. We both found other places to live during the second semester to the relief of our landlady.

As a newly emancipated male, I knew enough not to seal dough in a jar, but, as I related earlier, not enough to avoid adding a hot-milk mixture to yeast. The result of the latter error was a glob for which the only alternative was to be placed in a plastic bag and banished to the garbage. Nevertheless, for a number of mistakes, I learned, by trial and error, a means of salvaging the dish without reducing its palatability excessively.

BREAD DOUGHS

When mixing ingredients for bread doughs with an electric mixer, do not add more than about ½ of flour. Otherwise the dough will climb the beaters and make an awful mess of the mixer. Add the remaining ½ of flour and mix with a wooden spoon.

CREAM SAUCES

A variety of recipes listed herein call for a mixture of flour or corn starch, milk, sometimes some kind of fat, and perhaps broth or the water in which some vegetable was steamed. In some instances the flour is added to the fat and mixed, then the cold milk and other ingredients added ,whereas in other recipes a mixture of corn starch in cold water is added to the heated milk. The mixtures are cooked, stirring continuously, until they become thick and bubbly. Only sometimes they become bubbly, but not very thick and in other instances they become like glue even before the first bubble forms. What to do? No need to start over. If too thick, add a bit of cold water or milk and continue to stir; if too thin, mix ½ tablespoon of cornstarch in ⅛th cup of **COLD** water, add to the mixture and continue to stir. Voil! The recipe is saved.

LIGHTER CAKES

For very light cakes, both those made from recipes herein and those prepared from commercial mixes, let the batter sit in the baking pan while the oven heats (5–6 minutes). This gives time for the soda or baking powder to begin to work. However, if you delay baking too long, the cake will be so tender that it becomes difficult to eat with a dessert fork. If that happens, get a spoon, add a little frozen yogurt and enjoy!

COOKING PASTA

When cooking pasta, add 1–2 tablespoons of olive oil to the water. It tends to keep excessive amounts of foam from forming on the surface of the water late in the cooking process that sometimes causes the water to boil over. It also imparts a good taste to the pasta.

MIXING SAUCES

Normal procedure is to mix flour and oil, then add milk in making many sauces. Once, I put the flour in the pan and added milk and began to heat the mix without adding oil with the flour. In hopes of salvaging the sauce, I quickly added the oil on top of the milk. Quick and extensive use of a wisk created a sauce indistinguishable from that produced the normal way.

MIXING CAKES, PANCAKES, AND OTHER DISHES WITH BOTH WET AND DRY INGREDIENTS

Measure dry ingredients and add to the mixing bowl first, then measure and add wet ingredients. This permits using the same measuring cups and spoons without having to wash and dry them but once. When I was newly emancipated I frequently forgot to follow this axiom, but as a person who hates to wash dishes, I quickly learned that I could avoid lots of dishwashing by measuring things in this order. Also, if the recipe calls for both oil and egg substitute, measure the oil first as the residue of oil prevents the egg substitute from sticking to the measuring cup.

INDEX

Conversions

3 teaspoons = 1 tablespoon
2 tablespoons = ⅛ cup = 1 ounce
4 tablespoons = ¼ cup = 2 ounces
8 tablespoons = ½ cup = 4 ounces
16 tablespoons = 1 cup = ½ pint = 8 ounces
2 cups = 1 pint = 16 ounces
4 cups = 2 pints = 1 quart = 32 ounces
4 quarts = 1 gallon = 128 ounces

Equivalents

1 tablespoon corn starch (for thickening) = 2 tablespoons flour = 4 teaspoons quick-cooking tapioca
3 tablespoons baking cocoa + 1 tablespoon canola oil = 1 square (= 1 ounce) unsweetened baking cocoa
1 package or 2 teaspoons active dry yeast = 1 cake compressed yeast
1 egg white + ⅛ cup (= 2 tablespoons) egg substitute = 1 whole egg

For the following equivalents the dry portion can be added to dry ingredients and the wet portion can be added to wet ingredients within recipes:

2 teaspoons dried egg white + 2 tablespoons warm water or milk = 1 egg white
4 tablespoons dried cultured buttermilk + 1 cup water or milk = 1 cup liquid cultured buttermilk
¼ cup powdered milk + 1 cup water = 1 cup milk with ½% fat

Designers: Leslie N. & B. J. Verts
Compositor: Leslie N. Verts
Text: 12/14.4 Times New Roman, PageMaker 6.5, Windows 98
Display: Times New Roman, PageMaker 6.5, Windows 98
Printer and Binder: Cascade Printing Company, Corvallis, Oregon

NOTES